Social Entrepreneurship

_earning Resources
Centre

12773328

ISBN 0-9546673-0-1

Published by Senate Hall Academic Publishing

Editorial Office: Senate Hall Academic Publishing, PO Box 10689, Birmingham, B3 IWL, UK.

Tel: +44 121 233 3837
Fax: +44 121 233 3497
Email: info@senatehall.com
Website: http://www.senatehall.com

Administration: Senate Hall Academic Publishing, PO Box 8261, Shankil, Co. Dublin, Ireland.

Tel: +353 1 200 5066
Fax: +353 1 282 3701

CONTENTS

1. Introduction: New Perspectives on Social and Educational Entrepreneurship

Marilyn L. Kourilsky
UCLA

William B. Walstad
University of Nebraska - Lincoln

1. Introduction

This publication is both an edited volume and a special issue that is the product of a highly selective refereeing process. The rationale for the *International Journal of Entrepreneurship Education* (*IJEE*) Special Issue on Social (and Educational) Entrepreneurship, sponsored by the UCLA Institute for the Study of Educational Entrepreneurship (ISEE) and the Kauffman Foundation, originally emerged from a growing recognition that the worlds of social entrepreneurship and education are increasingly cross-pollinating. There are numerous examples and models, as will be explored in this set of articles, of how entrepreneurship is being used or can be used to enhance and support education at the pre-college level. This kindergarten through twelfth grade (K–12) education in the United States traditionally has been thought to be a public sector issue because the funding comes largely from government sources. Although there are private schools and initiatives in the United States, the vast majority of students are educated in public schools, and most of the funding for education comes from local, state, and federal government.

Government influence and control over education is no longer as dominant as it used to be. There are social innovations and powerful ideas coming from both the private for profit sector and the not-for-profit sector that are challenging existing ways of structuring and providing education for students. These changes also are stimulating the adoption of more entrepreneurial practices in the operations of public schools. Such efforts are being undertaken to make K–12 education more dynamic and effective, and also to make it more self-supporting and efficient. Most academic research, however, has only tangentially investigated this topic, and tends to focus on either education or entrepreneurship instead of the interaction between the two fields. This set of articles makes the connections between the two separate, but related areas. They were written to illustrate new ideas and stimulate new thinking about social entrepreneurship in general, about how education can be more enterprising, and about how entrepreneurship can strengthen educational institutions and practices.

The editors of the Special Issue formulated two broad questions to be addressed by the Issue's papers.

1. Can "social impact" be compatible with "for profit" wealth creation? How does a social entrepreneur manage the tradeoffs? Under what circumstances are both goals aligned, and under what conditions are they in conflict?

2. What is the potential impact of educational entrepreneurship (both for profit and not-for-profit) on public school reform in general, and on urban school reform in particular? What are some of the key issues to consider?

The editors then conducted an exhaustive search for scholars in the United States who had or could best answer these questions and improve our understanding of social and educational entrepreneurship. Seven individuals or teams of scholars were selected to prepare papers for the Special Issue. These papers were circulated in their draft stages so that all the authors and a team of referees could read them and offer comments. Based on this feedback and on detailed commentary by the Issue's editors, authors made additional revisions to meet the particular requirements and standards of the Issue. It is this rigorous process of selection, review, and revision that produced this *IJEE* Special Issue's set of articles on social and educational entrepreneurship.

2. The Articles

The first three articles in this Issue by Gregory Dees and Beth Anderson (2003), Calvin Kent and Lorraine Anderson (2003), and William Walstad (2003) focus primarily on the first Special Issue question about the compatibility of social impact and for-profit wealth creation. Although they explain how entrepreneurship and entrepreneurial thinking may be used to serve a social purpose that improves communities and society, each article offers a different perspective on social entrepreneurship. The next four articles by Paul Hill (2003), Henry Levin (2003), Ted Kolderie (2003), and Marilyn Kourilsky and Guilbert Hentschke (2003) target the second main question. They investigate the potential for using entrepreneurship in education to provide K–12 educational reform. These articles present different examples of such educational initiatives and consider their potential for improving elementary and secondary education. What follows is a brief synopsis of each article to describe how each article contributes to our understanding of social and educational entrepreneurship.

2.1. Dees and Anderson

Dees and Anderson address the question of whether the wealth-creation imperative inherent in for-profit organizations is really compatible with optimal social impact. They begin by focusing on social entrepreneurs, who they define as individuals creating enterprises that are intended to serve society and make a profit at the same time. They note the growing importance of this type of entrepreneurship: "as traditional sector boundaries continue to break down, there will be a rise in the number of social entrepreneurs who want to combine a social purpose with a for-profit organizational structure." They define for-profit social ventures as legally incorporated for-profit entities explicitly designed to serve a social purpose. The article makes a clear distinction between for-profit social ventures and other types of social ventures such as not-for-profit business ventures, socially responsible businesses, and purely profit-motivated firms operating in the social sector.

Dees and Anderson use a "value chain" concept as a tool for analyzing potential sources of competitive advantage for a firm. The simplified value chain, which includes procurement, employment, production, product or service, and marketing, is used to highlight major activities through which a business can create social value. The potential benefits of combining social purpose with a profit motive include such factors as promoting efficiency and innovation, leveraging scarce public and philanthropic resources, responding quickly to demand, and improving access to skills personnel.

The creation of a for-profit social venture is not without many challenges. These challenges can arise from the complexity of combining two very different kinds of objectives. There also can be market pressures to compromise on social value creation or there can be political pressures to compromise on financial performance. The authors assert that these challenges can be met, and they offer eight strategies.

1. Be clear and open about the venture's mission, including both social and economic objectives.

2. Articulate a comprehensive venture model that integrates a plausible social impact theory with a viable business model.

3. Be creative in measuring performance and ruthless in testing the assumptions behind the venture model.

4. Start with sympathetic investors and retain control in the hands of those who are committed to the dual mission.

5. Invest time and energy in hiring and developing the right people.

6. Anticipate resistance and develop a strategy for dealing with it.

7. Develop a brand reputation for quality and performance.

8. Recognize the limits of what can be done for profit and use not-for-profit partners or affiliates to provide complementary services.

Dees and Anderson conclude that for-profit social entrepreneurs can succeed if they follow these strategies. Such work will require them to be "tenacious" in following their social and economic goals and also "flexible" in finding viable ways to achieve them.

2.2. Kent and Anderson

Kent and Anderson offer a different perspective on social entrepreneurship by focusing on the importance of social capital and its relationship to entrepreneurship and leadership. They lament that the study of entrepreneurship in business schools thus far has been limited primarily to technology and the ventures that produce it. They argue that innovation is more than new products and processes for production because entrepreneurs can be the change agents for creating social as well as material progress. In making their case, they define social capital as "the stock of active connections among people; the trust, mutual understanding and shared values and behaviors that bind the members of human networks and communities and make cooperative action possible." They further explain that social capital has both internal and external dimensions. Internally, social capital increases the effectiveness of the organization by establishing a workplace where workers are encouraged to create. Externally, social capital increases the effectiveness of social institutions in pursuing greater social harmony, through an interdisciplinary approach that engages sociological, political and economic issues.

Kent and Anderson observe that social capital has an economic value because knowledge creates a competitive advantage. They make a distinction between information and knowledge: the former being sterile data which can easily be transformed; the latter being the human skills necessary to understand the data, assimilate it and apply it in new and creative ways. In their view, social capital depends foremost on trust, and trust necessarily comes from human interaction. Social capital therefore has an economic value also because transaction costs are reduced when people trust each other. They assert that the stronger a social community is, the greater the level of trust there is between its members. Trust encourages risk-taking by reducing the fear of failure. Risk-taking in turn yields greater innovation and more entrepreneurship. Successful businesses, therefore, are built on trust between company and customer, employer and employee, and employees and their colleagues.

The authors also see a strong relationship between leadership and social capital. They make an important distinction between management and leadership: the former tending to yield consistent results or the status quo; the latter having the potential to produce dramatic change. Effective leadership requires the ability to develop a vision for the future and to motivate others to work towards the accomplishment of that goal. The authors highlight the concept of "servant leadership" in which leaders think of themselves as working for their employees in terms of supporting whatever they need (e.g., materials, training, encouragement, rewards, recognition). They also note that leaders need to be honest with their employees, praising them for their accomplishments while providing them with honest feedback. Similarly, entrepreneurs need to give as much attention to their co-workers as they do to a new idea. An effective entrepreneur understands that through strong relationships built on trust, great accomplishments naturally follow.

This article finishes with several recommendations for changes in the curricula of business schools. They think that these schools should give more emphasis to social capital in the education of future entrepreneurs and business leaders. Students need to understand the importance of developing social communities based on shared values and goals because they create trust, and it is this trust that is the basis for entrepreneurial risk-taking, product innovation, and economic growth.

2.3. Walstad

Walstad offers a third perspective on social entrepreneurship. His article describes the multiple effects of entrepreneurship that, when added together, have an enormous influence on society and education. These effects initially arise from the new product and innovations created by entrepreneurs, but there are other long-lasting effects on society that stem from the philanthropy created by entrepreneurs. The contribution that entrepreneurship makes to philanthropy serves as a foundation for most social entrepreneurship.

He begins by describing the direct and indirect effects of entrepreneurship on philanthropy. The direct effects came from the wealth created by the entrepreneur. He states that "entrepreneurs do not start out to become philanthropists, but they often assume that role when the business becomes successful." He then cites numerous examples of successful entrepreneurs, such as Bill Gates currently or Andrew Carnegie long before him, who became major philanthropists after amassing great fortunes. These fortunes have been used to influence and change society during the lifetime of successful entrepreneurs and long afterwards. In addition, there are associates of the entrepreneur and investors in entrepreneurial firms who also become wealthy and make additional contributions to philanthropy. These indirect effects expand the pool of wealth far beyond the business founder. For-profit wealth creation is clearly compatible with social impact when it gets channeled through philanthropy.

The article also describes a feedback effect from entrepreneurship that can be self-reinforcing. In the first link, entrepreneurship promotes increased philanthropy. In the second link, more philanthropy can improve society, and also education, as one of the main beneficiaries of this philanthropic spending. In the third link, a better society and educational system can encourage more entrepreneurship. He notes that this last connection between an improved society and increased entrepreneurship is the most tenuous of the three links in the model. He argues that this link can be strengthened when improvements in society and education lead to improvements in the business climate that supports entrepreneurship. Philanthropy can contribute to improving the business climate by helping potential entrepreneurs in underserved communities gain access to start-up capital, by providing effective programs in entrepreneurship education at all age levels, and by reducing the tax and regulatory costs that can serve as impediments for starting and growing businesses.

Walstad then discusses the other effects of entrepreneurship on society when analyzing what happens to the net worth of entrepreneurs. In addition to contributing to philanthropy, the net worth of entrepreneurs gets redistributed to society in other ways. Taxes are paid on entrepreneurial income and they fund public goods and services. The spending for consumption goods largely has personal effects, but there are social effects from the creation of jobs and the taxes paid on that consumption. Those family members who inherit the fortune of an entrepreneur will ultimately redistribute their inherited wealth through the same avenues: philanthropy, taxes, consumption expenditures and inheritance. He argues that all four of these avenues have an impact on society.

The final effect described in the article is the innovation effect on philanthropy from entrepreneurial giving. New approaches to charitable giving have encouraged wealthy entrepreneurs and traditional philanthropists to be more innovative about how best to make the nonprofit sector more accountable and create more social value from philanthropic funding. From this perspective, entrepreneurship has the power to radically transform society through philanthropy because it allows a wider diversity and flexibility of ideas, choices and programs to improve society as compared to government legislation and funding. Education will always be a main target of such activity because there is substantial spending on education by private foundations. As more entrepreneurs are created and successfully amass greater wealth, they will develop new, innovative approaches to redistributing their wealth to find the best way to benefit society and education.

2.4. Hill

The Hill article turns directly to the issue of educational entrepreneurship and, in particular, the changes needed to reform K–12 education in the United States. The thesis of this article is that public education is hurt by the lack of entrepreneurship, and that greater openness to entrepreneurship could make public education more adaptable and efficient. Hill thinks that education is plagued with uncertainty, and claims that the only two things which are certain in education are that not every child will learn best from the same form of instruction and when today's children are adults they will need to know things that few, if any, members of their parents' generation know. He thinks that the best mechanism for coping with such uncertainty is entrepreneurship. He utilizes Schumpeter's definition of entrepreneurship as the implementation of change via the introduction of new or better quality goods; new methods of production; new sources of supply; or reorganization of an industry.

In the first section, Hill describes the areas in which public education is weakened by being closed to entrepreneurship. Public education has little incentive or capacity to invest in new ideas, which results in public education not being able to adapt to demographic changes and seldom being able to take advantage of ideas and resources available in the broader society. The public school system, relative to most other American institutions, also does not do a good job of performing many important functions, such as quality control, the creation of new products, reaction to competition, staff recruitment and development, and financial control. Hill contends that within the public education system, no one has significant discretion over who is hired, where they are assigned, or how money is spent. As a result, potential entrepreneurs are regularly thwarted by a system bound by odd rules and customs.

In the second section, Hill considers how public education could be opened to entrepreneurship and thinks the key is discretion. If entrepreneurs are to change public education, people within the system must become capable of making real choices and reallocating real money. He recommends that this discretion be achieved with policies that eliminate any routine funding for central administrative units, and by allocating money to schools based on enrollment. Vouchers, charters and school contracting movements all make the flow of funds to schools transparent, allowing schools the freedom to buy what they need from a competitive marketplace of vendors. This would in turn encourage school leaders and teachers to become entrepreneurs with the incentive to constantly promote student learning. Hill suggests that a less radical-sounding proposal is standards-based reform which would similarly allow schools to control their funding, spending, hiring, use of time and selection of instructional methods, as long as they meet their performance expectations.

In the final section, Hill explains what would be the greatest opportunities for education entrepreneurs, once the laws governing public education are changed to allow money to follow children and individual schools are given discretion to make spending decisions. Four major areas for entrepreneurial innovation would be providing support services, managing human resources, delivering complete courses and operating whole schools. He concludes that entrepreneurship is needed in every aspect of school and system operations to free a public education system that is currently frozen by laws, regulations and labor contracts.

2.5. Levin

Levin presents a more circumspect and skeptical assessment of the potential of for-profit schools to reform K–12 education in the United States. His article begins with a brief history of this education to highlight the absence of for-profit schools as an important force in the development of the K–12 educational system. This observation suggests that there is something inherent about education that does not lend itself well to for-profit operations. In recent years, however, there has been a rise in educational management organizations (EMOs) that has re-inserted for-profit firms into elementary and secondary education. His article examines whether these for-profit EMOs have the potential to reform public education by asking whether EMOs can succeed as a business and if EMOs can stimulate changes that will lead to educational improvement.

In the case of the first question, Levin concludes that it is difficult for EMOs to turn a profit because the proponents of educational privatization failed to carefully study the economics or politics of education. Levin identifies five critical characteristics of education that those who decided to enter the "business of education" failed to realize: 1) education is a difficult business in which to make a profit because it is highly regulated and monitored, and also influenced by multiple groups and levels of government; 2) EMOs have marketing costs that must be paid to attract and sign charter schools and districts to contracts, but the public schools do not have such costs; 3) the contracts for EMOs are relatively short (3–5 years) which means that the overhead and startup costs on such contracts have to be amortized over a relatively short period of time; 4) the economies of scale that might appear to be present in operating many schools and teaching large numbers of students may be more elusive than real; 5) the push for uniformity across school sites does not take into account the important differences in educational needs within communities and may be difficult to achieve given these local differences. All of these factors lead Levin to conclude that the economic health of for-profit EMO firms is highly questionable and they are not likely to serve as viable business models.

For the second question, Levin considered two hypotheses of how for-profit EMOs potentially could promote educational reform. He first asked whether for-profit EMOs could operate schools that make organizational or pedagogical breakthroughs that might be emulated by public schools. In evaluating the research evidence, Levin found mixed results in terms of "revolutionary" breakthroughs by EMOs. There was no evidence of major positive benefits from EMOs with respect to improvement in curriculum, instructional strategies, or use of technologies, but there was strong evidence of improvement in the areas of personnel and organizational practices. The second hypothesis he evaluated was whether the EMOs might create competition between EMOs and public schools that would stimulate the latter to improve their operations. In this case, Levin found no direct or substantive evidence that EMOs spurred competition in public schools and improved results for the educational system.

Levin concludes that the present model of for-profit EMOs is not likely to be successful because they generally have not been profitable thus far and there is little evidence of breakthroughs in educational results. In the spirit of supporting educational entrepreneurship, Levin does offer selected recommendations that might make EMOs more successful than has been the case to date. He thinks that for-profit EMOs might work better as smaller firms that operate just a few schools, and that they should seek to establish themselves in niche markets such as special education. He also recommends that EMOs get better control over their administrative costs when operating multiple schools, and contain their marketing and promotional costs. Another recommendation is that EMOs negotiate longer contracts so that the high fixed costs of startup can be more easily amortized. Levin ends with the cautionary note that it will not be easy to create a network of for-profit EMOs in the United States because the private sector has not been successful in creating or penetrating the potential market.

2.6. Kolderie

Kolderie considers another approach to educational entrepreneurship and sees teachers as the key group with the power to transform K–12 educational institutions. His article discusses teacher ownership as a new form of educational entrepreneurship that has considerable potential to change the structure and practices of these institutions. Teacher cooperatives or partnerships allow teachers to make changes and improvements in education that so far have been impossible through the traditional school structures. In these arrangements teachers are no longer just employees but now have ownership in an educational institution and more interest in seeing it succeed.

He begins by describing why it is impossible for entrepreneurship to have an effect on education without first rearranging the education institution. He then states that the advent of "chartering" has allowed the traditional arrangements to be challenged and reinvented. The opportunity to open and operate charter schools has created a market for the services of entrepreneurs because the "buyer" of educational services is no longer limited to a political body. Furthermore, the charter sector serves as a research and development sector within K–12 education because it contains incentives for schools to operate in different ways. Kolderie defines an incentive as a reason combined with an opportunity and argues that the charter school sector contains both the reason and opportunity for educational reform. The charter school sector is the nation's major experiment with school-based decision-making because a charter school is responsible for managing its budget, selecting its teachers, managing its facilities and support services, and establishing its learning program.

Kolderie next describes teacher cooperatives as one kind of entrepreneurship that has manifested as a result of the growth of the charter school sector. He provides the example of the Minnesota New Country School that has a collection of contracts for transportation, extracurricular, lunch, facility and instructional services. It has a contract with EdVisions, a teacher cooperative, to provide the learning program. The teachers of EdVisions select their colleagues, decide on the instructional methods and materials, evaluate performance and decide their own compensation. At New Country School, the teachers have elected to have virtually all learning be project-based. EdVisions currently operates in 11 different schools. The Bill & Melinda Gates Foundation also invested \$4.5 million in 2000 to have this model replicated in 15 more schools over the next four years.

Kolderie concludes that the idea of teacher ownership is generalizable to other areas of K–12 education. He states that the traditional arrangement, in which teachers work as employees for administrators, is not essential to education. He also thinks that teacher ownership has significant implications for changing and improving K–12 education. It allows teachers to assume multiple professional roles as teachers, managers, and owners. Teacher practices are changed, and these changes have the potential to improve student learning. Teacher ownership can expand the supply of quality teachers by making teaching more attractive and rewarding. It can speed the introduction of learning technologies into the educational system. Finally, teacher ownership will help contain the costs of education while maintaining program quality.

2.7. Kourilsky and Hentschke

The concluding article by Kourilsky and Hentschke completes the discussion of educational entrepreneurship and its many possibilities by introducing the concept of "educational multisectorism." It involves drawing on the resources and strengths of all three economic sectors – private not-for-profit, private for profit, and public/government sectors – to provide significant benefits for the pursuit of educational reform. The authors contend this multisectorism is needed rather than just unisectorism, and that if entrepreneurial thinking and social entrepreneurship are used to implement the multisectorism then it can become a powerful paradigm for innovation and change.

Kourilsky and Hentschke begin by defining educational entrepreneurship and discussing how manifestations of educational entrepreneurship may vary with the three levels of the entrepreneurial spectrum pyramid: entrepreneurship, entrepreneurial behavior, and entrepreneurism. They then describe the evolutionary changes that are fostering the growth of educational entrepreneurship in K–12 education: 1) increasing publicly expressed dissatisfaction with public education, 2) increasing reliance on multiple sources of revenue, 3) changing organizational frameworks: from centralized public models to decentralized market models, 4) increasing inter-penetration by education service providers of historically protected markets, 5) changing relationships between the 'policy end' and the 'operation end' as educational organizations move from compliance to performance, and 6) increasing reliance on technology for service delivery, organization and operation.

The next section of the article focuses on the education "industry" today, highlighting its historical antecedents, the current trends that are shaping it, and its expanded modern presence well beyond traditional schools, colleges, and universities. Kourilsky and Hentschke note that as K–12 education rapidly evolves into a three-sector domain, each sector enjoys certain comparative advantages relative to various types of educational objectives, organizations and ventures. The government or public sector has a comparative advantage in the areas of core learning, social justice initiatives, and holistic anchoring of the student. The private not-for-profit sector has a comparative advantage in the areas of core value (filling unmet social needs), having access to the "hearts" of individuals and organizations that value K–12 education, and filling gaps left by public market failures. The private for-profit sector has a comparative advantage in the areas of identifying market niches, accessing capital for investment, and building compelling and innovative business models. The private sector (both not-for-profit and for profit sectors) also has comparative advantages in providing specialty services for education, alternatives to existing public schools (e.g., charter schools and teacher cooperatives), and laboratories for educational innovation.

Kourilsky and Hentschke observe that entrepreneurship and entrepreneurial thinking can emerge in any sector of an economy. In the not-for-profit private sector, the main focus is on the social mission for education and how best to achieve effects in the targeted areas of social need. In the for-profit private sector, the pursuit of the social mission has to be balanced responsibly against the economic obligations of the venture. In the public sector, the social mission of education is the main focus but there is the additional need to provide acceptable levels of service for governmental jurisdictions. They make the case that the most successful K–12 educational leaders will be "innovative, opportunity-oriented, resourceful, value-creating change agents" who pursue their social mission across sector lines and use the strengths of each sector.

3. Conclusion

Entrepreneurship has tremendous power to transform and change society. The conventional view is that entrepreneurship is about startup businesses and the contribution they make to economic growth. This set of articles, however, shows that entrepreneurship should be conceived more broadly and has wide applicability to important social concerns. One pressing concern is how best to reform K–12 education in the United States to make it more dynamic, innovative, and effective. This set of articles explores how entrepreneurship directed to a social or educational purpose potentially can improve education. Although the answers vary and the articles cover a range of topics, this special issue should provide new insights about the potential for entrepreneurship and entrepreneurial practices to advance educational reform.

2. For-Profit Social Ventures

J. Gregory Dees and Beth Battle Anderson

Duke University

Abstract. Traditional sector boundaries are breaking down as societies search for more innovative, cost-effective, and sustainable ways to solve social problems and provide socially important goods, such as education and health care. One result has been a rise in the number of social entrepreneurs who want to combine a social purpose with a for-profit organizational structure. Is the wealth-creation imperative inherent in for-profit organizations really compatible with optimal social impact? This paper is designed to help would-be for-profit social entrepreneurs understand and address the challenges of using a for-profit organization to serve a social objective. Drawing on a wide range of literature as well as case studies, we identify the challenges facing for-profit social ventures and outline strategies for responding. Of course, there are limits to what can be done within a for-profit structure. Our analysis should help social entrepreneurs recognize those limits and respond to them intelligently as they design their organizations.

Keywords: social entrepreneurship, social enterprise, social purpose business, social impact, social ventures, social sector, entrepreneurship.

1. Introduction

We live in an age in which the boundaries between the government, nonprofit, and business sectors are blurring.[1] This blurring results from a search for more innovative, cost-effective, and sustainable ways to address social problems and deliver socially important goods, such as basic education and health care. Much of the action revolves around experiments using business practices and structures to serve social objectives. Increasingly, government agencies and nonprofit organizations are adopting frameworks, methods, and strategies from the business world in hopes of improving their performance. More dramatically, for-profit organizations are emerging or expanding their presence in arenas formerly dominated by nonprofit or government providers, often with the blessing and encouragement of public officials. This boundary blurring has led to a new breed of social entrepreneurs creating for-profit organizations explicitly to serve social purposes.

But does it make sense to blend the profit motive with a social objective? Adam Smith was skeptical. In concluding one of his most famous passages about the "invisible hand," Smith (1776) makes the following observation

---

1. For treatment of the blurring sector, see Ryan (1999) and Dees and Anderson (2003).

about business people, "I have never known much good done by those who affected to trade for the public good. It is an affection, indeed, not very common among merchants, and very few words need be employed in dissuading them from it (p. 478)." Even those who do not share Smith's skepticism must admit that successful examples are rare and the risks of conflict between pursuing profit and serving a social objective are significant. How can wealth creation be aligned with serving a social purpose and doing it well? This paper aims to help social entrepreneurs who are interested in pursuing a social purpose within a for-profit structure answer that question.

2. Defining For-Profit Social Ventures

In this paper, we are concerned with *for-profit social ventures*, defined as entrepreneurial organizations that are:

1. *Legally incorporated as for-profit entities*, with one or more owners who have a formal right to control the firm and who are entitled to its residual earnings and net assets. For-profit forms include proprietorships, partnerships, corporations, limited liability companies, and cooperatives.

2. *Explicitly designed to serve a social purpose* while making a profit. Having a social purpose involves a commitment to creating value for a community or society rather than just wealth for the owners or personal satisfaction for customers.

For-profit social ventures measure their success in terms of social impact. However, given their choice of the for-profit structure, they must pay close attention to the creation of economic value as well. Thus, whether they view economic value as a means for creating social value or as inherently valuable on its own, for-profit social entrepreneurs have dual social and financial objectives that guide their managerial decision-making and determine their success. This goal is commonly referred to as the "double bottom line."

It is important to distinguish for-profit social ventures from three related types of enterprises that we are not addressing in this paper:

Nonprofit business ventures. Increasingly, nonprofit organizations are operating commercial enterprises within their nonprofit structure. While similar to for-profit social ventures in their objectives and operations, nonprofits are legally prevented from distributing economic surplus. They are also free to use philanthropic support to subsidize their start-up costs and their on-going operations. Thus, they do not face the same capital markets and profit pressures as for-profit social ventures.

Socially responsible businesses. A socially responsible business achieves commercial success in ways that respect ethical values, people, communities, and the environment.[2] These businesses may even provide resources to and actively engage with public or nonprofit organizations to serve a specific social cause. However, unlike for-profit social ventures, their primary goal is the creation of economic value.

Purely profit-motivated firms operating in the social sector. The boundary blurring of recent years has seen some firms enter the social sector simply in search of profits. These organizations typically do not place inherent value on the social impact they create. Thus, Lockheed Martin's entry into the welfare-to-work arena in order to increase profitability through diversification does not qualify the firm as a social purpose venture.

While our focus is on enterprises that deliberately set out to create social value within a for-profit organizational structure, we may draw on lessons learned in these other categories to inform entrepreneurs who truly want to combine the profit motive with a social purpose.

3. Variations on the Theme

A for-profit venture may pursue its social goals in many different ways. These various methods can be organized around key stages in the business value chain. Strategist Michael Porter (1985) introduced the "value chain" concept as a tool for analyzing potential sources of competitive advantage for a firm. It includes all the activities through which businesses can create economic value, from purchasing raw materials to providing after-sales service. A simplified form of the value chain helps identify the major activities through which a business can create social value.

Figure 1: The Simplified Social Value Chain

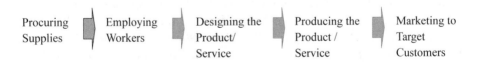

| Procuring Supplies | Employing Workers | Designing the Product/ Service | Producing the Product / Service | Marketing to Target Customers |

2.   Adapted from the mission of Business for Social Responsibility, http://www.bsr.org.

Procurement. Entrepreneurs can use their purchasing practices to serve social purposes. The most common practices involve purchasing from disadvantaged suppliers or engaging in environmentally friendly purchasing. For example, one of many "fair trade" organizations, Café Campesino provides specialty coffees by only purchasing coffee grown in socially and environmentally responsible ways, from democratically managed, small-scale farmer cooperatives in Mexico and Latin America. Another for-profit social venture, Recycline develops and delivers to market quality products from recycled materials, initially producing recyclable toothbrushes made from 100% recycled plastic.

Employment. Employment practices can be similarly used for social purposes. One common strategy is to employ disadvantaged individuals (such as people with disabilities, drug addicts, ex-convicts, homeless teens, etc.) with the goal of providing training and development opportunities. For instance, Cooperative Home Care Associates was established to create high quality paraprofessional jobs for low-income women that simultaneously empower the women and improve the quality of the home health care industry. Currently, CHCA employs over 550 African-American and Latina women, 75% of whom had been dependent on public assistance. Average wages and benefits are among the highest in the industry, worker turnover is significantly lower than industry average, and nearly 80% of CHCA's employees with over one year's seniority share in the cooperative's ownership.[3]

Product or Service. Certain products or services have inherent social value. Consider basic K-12 education, which has private benefits for consumers but also benefits society at large. Operating in this industry, LearnNow strives to provide youth from under-resourced communities with a world-class education, certainly benefiting the students, but also helping to produce responsible citizens and leaders for the future. Other examples in this category include products that are more environmentally sustainable or are aimed at alleviating a major social problem, such as hunger, crime, or drug addiction.

Production. Entrepreneurs can also use their methods of producing and delivering their goods to serve a social purpose. Environmentally friendly production practices provide the most common example. For instance, Green Mountain Energy Company provides 500,000 customers with "cleaner electricity" from sources such as wind, solar, water, and cleaner burning natural gas. Energy producers that use renewable sources not only reduce pollution and its associated problems, but they also decrease our dependency

---

3.   See Dawson, Steven L., and Sherman, L. Kreiner, "Cooperative Home Care Associates: History and Lessons," Home Health Associates Training Institute, January 1993 and information retrieved 5/22/2002 from National Network of Sector Partners, http://www.nedlc.org/nnsp/practitioners/chca.html.

on foreign oil as well as the need for drilling in environmentally sensitive areas.

Marketing to Target Customers. Entrepreneurs can serve a social purpose by targeting a particularly disadvantaged market in a way that not only benefits individuals in that market, but also benefits society. Providing housing to the homeless, family planning for the rural poor, and food to the needy fall into this category. One prominent example involves providing credit to disadvantaged small business owners who would otherwise not have access to capital. Grameen Bank pioneered this concept in Bangladesh over twenty years ago by profitably extending credit to landless poor, primarily women, who had no credit history or assets to secure these loans but rarely defaulted due to the success of peer-lending groups that evaluated, monitored, and supported the borrowers.

Because for-profit social ventures are so diverse in their social purposes and their methods of operation, we have to be careful in making generalizations. Many challenges will vary depending on where in the value chain social entrepreneurs aim to create social value. However, for this paper, we will keep our focus sufficiently general to be helpful to any social entrepreneurs who want to serve a social purpose through a for-profit structure, regardless of their chosen method.

4. Potential Benefits of For-Profit Social Ventures

Social entrepreneurs may be drawn to for-profit structures in part for personal reasons. They may want to see if they can "do well" while at the same time "doing good." For-profit enterprises offer a potential financial upside that exceeds the financial rewards commonly found in the social sector. However, oftentimes the motivation goes beyond personal rewards. Many social entrepreneurs believe that for-profit structures have virtues that are not easily mimicked by nonprofit or public sector counterparts. These potential benefits tend to fall into five categories.

Promoting efficiency and innovation. The profit motive, if properly channeled, has the potential to encourage efficiency and innovation. For-profit organizations generally are driven to maximize every dollar of investment and minimize expenses incurred in creating and delivering value. At the same time, they have incentives to discover innovative, cost-effective ways of achieving their objectives.

Leveraging scarce public and philanthropic resources. The presence of for-profit providers can also be seen as a way to leverage scarce social resources, allowing philanthropic and tax dollars to be directed to where they are most needed. For-profit social ventures, if sufficiently profitable, can tap into private capital markets for investment funds. Some of them will also draw on private revenue sources to fund at least a portion of their activities. By occupying niches and serving markets for which the profit potential is high, they can free public and philanthropic resources to focus on those niches, segments, and programs that need subsidies.

Responding quickly to demand. Researchers have reported that for-profit organizations are more responsive to fluctuations in market demand than are their nonprofit counterparts. As Henry Hansmann (1996) points out,

> The empirical evidence indicates fairly clearly that, when demand increases rapidly in the human services, nonprofit firms respond by entering or increasing their capacity only slowly; for-profit firms are much quicker in entering or expanding to fill the gap.... Similarly, nonprofit firms appear to be slow to reduce their output, or to withdraw from an industry entirely, when demand for their services contracts. (p. 249)

This market responsiveness can be an advantage for spreading innovations in a timely manner, re-allocating resources when appropriate, and dealing with social needs that are expected to vary over time.

Improving access to skilled personnel. For-profit social ventures also have the potential to expand the labor pool by attracting people with skills that are also highly valued in business. Nonprofit and public sector organizations often have a difficult time competing with the business world for managerial and technical talent, and talented individuals often leave the sectors out of frustration or when their family obligations grow more onerous. By custom, nonprofit and governmental salaries are traditionally lower and cannot be augmented by the potential upside associated with equity ownership. For-profit social ventures can appeal to skilled personnel who might otherwise leave or fail to consider working in the social sector because of the limited financial rewards or other perceived limitations associated with working in nonprofit or government jobs.

Note that we did not mention the popular notion of financial "sustainability" in our list of benefits. We see no compelling evidence that for-profit organizations have greater chances of survival than nonprofits or public agencies. Business failure rates are relatively high, and we have no reason to believe that for-profit social ventures will be immune to the forces and factors that lead so many business ventures to fail. However, the potential benefits outlined above may provide compelling reasons for social entrepreneurs to adopt a for-profit structure.

5. Challenges of Combining Social Purpose with a Profit Motive

Of course, for-profit structures bring with them potential problems that may offset their benefits. Market forces and potential incentive problems can lead even the best-intentioned social entrepreneurs astray. Successful social entrepreneurs need to understand and address the challenges of combining the profit motive with social objectives in a way that still preserves at least some of the benefits that make the for-profit structure attractive in the first place. In attempting to do so, for-profit social entrepreneurs should be particularly aware of the additional complexity that arises when combining two different, sometimes divergent, objectives, as well as the potential pressures to compromise one or both of their objectives.

5.1. Complexity of Combining Two Very Different Kinds of Objectives

Making decisions and building an effective organization are inevitably more complicated with two objectives rather than one, particularly when they are different in some fundamental ways.

Differences in metrics and measurability affect management decision-making and external credibility. Though some social benefits can be converted into purely dollar terms,[4] many important social purposes defy this kind of economic translation, making direct comparison of financial and social performance difficult. Furthermore, not only are financial and social objectives often incommensurable, but social objectives are also much more difficult to measure. Social benefits are often intangible, hard to quantify, difficult to attribute to a specific organization, best evaluated in the future, and open to dispute. This measurement problem plagues the nonprofit sector and is equally confounding for for-profit social ventures where entrepreneurs and managers are attempting to make bottom line decisions based on both economic and social impact. This imbalance presents obstacles to making optimal managerial decisions, while also making it difficult to produce compelling evidence of social impact.

It is extremely hard to make strategic decisions about resource allocation or practical cost/quality tradeoffs when the social impact of these decisions is nearly impossible to measure in an efficient, timely, and reliable fashion. It can become all too easy to focus too heavily on the more familiar, tangible and straightforward economic measures of success. At the same time, uncertainty around demonstrated social impact makes it especially difficult to assess how much to invest in pursuing a particular means of creating social value or achieving a certain quality of social goods or services.

---

4. The best work on converting social benefits into dollar terns is the "social return on investment" work done by the Roberts Enterprise Development Fund, see http:// www.redf.org. However, even this work captures only "system savings" and does not include other important dimensions of social benefit.

The absence of clear and reliable social impact measures also makes it difficult to demonstrate convincingly to key stakeholders the social benefit of a particular venture. This uncertainty may breed distrust on behalf of stakeholders, potentially exposing the venture to criticism. Without adequate information on social impact, customers and the general public may fear that for-profit providers will favor their personal profits over quality services. In fact, the contract-failure theory of the nonprofit firm argues that nonprofits enter the market precisely to mitigate the profit incentive and ensure that quality is not sacrificed in these situations (Hansmann, 1980). In some cases, the lack of uniformly accepted social impact measures might also provide grounds for dispute. Indeed, in the early years of the relationship between Baltimore City Schools and for-profit education management company Education Alternatives, Inc. (EAI), the teacher's union published negative reports on educational performance and expenditures that differed greatly from EAI's self-reported results. Each side repeatedly claimed the other was misrepresenting data, leaving the public confused (Dees & Elias, 1995). Moreover, once it became clear that EAI had published misleading results, given their profit motivation, there was greater stakeholder skepticism about whether they had done so intentionally or by mistake.

<u>Combining objectives from two different fields makes it difficult to build an integrated organization</u>. For-profit social ventures blend objectives that have been associated with two different fields of endeavor, business and the social sector. This combination makes organizational development a much greater challenge.

Hiring employees who can function well in both worlds is challenging. While increasingly individuals with nonprofit backgrounds and interests are seeking MBAs and getting business experience, this pool is still relatively small. Furthermore, there is no easy way for most social ventures to identify the rare candidates with the dual expertise they need. Community development financial institutions seek people with banking and community development expertise. Eco-tourism companies want to attract individuals who understand both ecology and the travel industry. A partner with Heidrick & Struggles International executive recruiting firm characterized the situation facing for-profit higher education companies this way:

> Companies are certainly nervous about hiring executives without educational experience, but they're also apprehensive about hiring managers directly from colleges and other nonprofit organizations for reasons they generally feel should be obvious. Namely, nonprofit executives tend not to appreciate the dynamics of making a profit. While this is a generalization that often proves inaccurate, it is equally matched by a tendency for those executives with backgrounds in higher education to minimize the challenges faced by emerging businesses (Haberman, 2001).

Because the combination is so rare, many for-profit social entrepreneurs build their teams by bringing together people from each side. However, this approach also has its challenges. Attracting people with skills valued in the business world can be difficult. In practice, the financial rewards available in a for-profit social venture may be better than those in typical nonprofit or government jobs, but they are generally still going to be less than those associated with traditional for-profit ventures. At the same time, individuals with the necessary social sector skills may be skeptical of the profit motive and thus more comfortable in a nonprofit or public sector environment. Even if social entrepreneurs can attract strong mixed teams, managing cultural differences may be difficult. Business-oriented employees are generally more used to taking risks, working in fast-paced environments, and setting clear, measurable goals and objectives. Individuals from the social sector are often more consensus-driven, passionate about a particular cause, and focused on responding to needs rather than anticipating or creating them. Establishing a culture and operating environment that values and thus successfully retains employees from both of these worlds is no easy task (Flannery & Deiglmeier, 1999).

5.2. Market Pressures to Compromise on Social Value Creation

In addition to the complexities of having dual objectives, competitive market pressures may drive out social preferences that are not economically efficient. Additionally, capital or customer markets may provide incentives to compromise on social value creation.

Competitive markets may drive out inefficient social preferences. Many economists argue that when a conflict between profits and social preferences arises, profits will dominate or the entrepreneur will be driven out of business. Milton Friedman (1962) makes this point forcefully:

> A businessman or entrepreneur who expresses preferences in his business activities that are not related to productive efficiency is at a disadvantage compared to other individuals who do not. Such an individual is in effect imposing higher costs on himself than are other individuals who do not have such preferences. Hence, in a free market they will tend to drive him out (p. 110).

Interestingly, Friedman is using this argument to make the case that markets will drive out racial discrimination. However, as illustrated more recently by William Baumol, the same reasoning applies to positive social preferences as well as negative ones. Baumol (1991) asserts, "Voluntary [socially-concerned] action leaves the business firm exposed and unprotected against the competitive advantage enjoyed by enterprises with less concerned (less ethical) managements" (p. 22). Moreover, taking social objectives seriously is likely to create at least opportunity costs by limiting the firm's choices.

Friedman and Baumol may overstate the case since real markets are not as competitive as those in economic models. Competitive markets did not drive out discrimination and may not completely drive out positive social objectives either. However, they do have force and generally do not reward or even tolerate substantial inefficiency. Thus, social objectives that create incremental costs for a venture may be difficult to sustain.

Consider the example of Community Products, Inc. (CPI), the original producer of Rainforest Crunch candy. CPI planned to source nuts from a Brazilian rain forest cooperative that harvested the nuts in an environmentally friendly way and employed rain forest residents. CPI promoted this aspect of its social mission extensively. However, CPI soon found that the cooperative could not meet the rapidly growing demand for the nuts and that some of the nuts received were spoiled and others were contaminated with bacteria. Without another socially comparable nut supplier, CPI had to make a choice. It could slow growth and incur the costs of helping to improve the quality of nuts from this supplier, which would significantly limit or even eliminate its profits. Or, it could bow to market pressures and buy nuts on the open market. CPI went with the market. This move undermined an important aspect of CPI's intended social impact and was a great embarrassment when it became public knowledge a few years later (Welles, 1998).

Investor expectations may undermine social value creation. Managing and meeting investor expectations regarding profit levels, growth, and liquidity can be a major challenge for the social entrepreneur. For-profit investors typically want a competitive return, which is a function of profit levels, perceived risk, and growth prospects. They also want an opportunity for liquidity – the ability to convert their investments into cash within a reasonable period of time. While Jed Emerson (2000) has argued that investors should look for a total return that includes financial and social returns, this idea has not yet caught on with the vast majority of investors. Even foundations that have a clear social mission invest most of their assets with the objective of generating high financial returns that can then be used to fund their grants. Return-oriented investors may pressure social ventures into actions that could harm the social mission. For example, the leaders of two for-profit education companies, LearnNow and Explore, Inc., wrestled with the question of how to balance investor desires for growth and scale with their commitment to deliver a quality product and serve their target social markets. There was demand for their services, but the rapid growth that was deemed necessary to generate sufficient returns to some investors posed risks to their social mission (Dees & Anderson, 2001; Grossman, Austin, Hart, & Peyus, 1999). After wrestling with this tension, both of these companies were acquired, LearnNow by publicly held Edison Schools, and Explore, Inc. by EdSolutions, Inc. The effect of the acquisitions on the social impact of these ventures remains to be seen.

Even customer preferences may lead social entrepreneurs astray. In most markets, customer pressure to deliver value is healthy. As Kenneth Arrow (1973) has pointed out, "On detailed analysis it appears the firm will find it privately profitable to reduce quality only if, in fact, quality reduction is a net social benefit, that is, if the saving in costs is worth more to the consumer than the quality reduction" (pp. 304-5). However, Arrow's logic applies only when the consumer is the payer, quality is transparent, and consumer value is commensurate with social benefit. In for-profit social ventures, frequently at least one of the following conditions holds, undermining the benevolent market logic described by Arrow:

- *Third-party payers have incentives that are not aligned with the firm's social mission or the interests of the firm's intended beneficiaries.*[5] Third-party payers are common in the social sector. Yet, often their interests do not perfectly align with creating the optimal social impact. For instance, political pressures on a public health agency may lead to lower payments for drug rehabilitation services than would be socially ideal. Firms competing to be the low cost provider may be pressured to compromise on social impact.

- *Relative quality is hard for paying customers to assess.* Given the difficulty measuring social value, customers often do not have adequate information to make decisions on the quality of social goods and services. Think of making a choice among different homeless shelters, social service agencies, or even nursing homes. Technology and third-party assessments are improving consumer decisions in some of these areas, but the quality of most social services remains far from transparent.[6] Thus, customer demand (or the lack thereof) is not a reliable indicator of whether social value is being produced efficiently or effectively.

- *Consumer value is not commensurate with social benefit.* Most social ventures intend to create societal benefits that go beyond what they might directly provide to the individuals they serve. In certain cases,

---

5. Sometimes third party payers are actually in a better position to assess quality than direct beneficiaries because they have a broader perspective and better access to performance data.
6. This is the premise of Henry Hansmann's economic theory of the nonprofit firm. See his classic article "The Role of Nonprofit Enterprise," *Yale Law Journal*, vol. 89, 1980, pp. 835-901.

the target community may resist the product or service being delivered because their adoption costs may exceed tangible benefits to them (Rangan, Karem, & Sandberg, 1996). Family planning services in developing countries represent a case in point. The market preferences of the potential consumers of these services are not a good indication of the social value of the services. Alternatively, high consumer demand need not indicate high social value. We may find a high level of demand for homeless shelters that serve alcoholic beverages, though this demand is no indication that these shelters are superior.

When any of these conditions hold, customer preferences (as reflected in market demand) will not serve as reliable indicators of social value creation. The prevalence of these conditions in any given social sector arena increases the risk that market pressures could lead even well intentioned social entrepreneurs into delivering less than optimal social impact.

5.3. Social and Political Pressures to Compromise on Financial Performance

Any enterprise that is openly driven by a social purpose may also find itself under pressure to severely limit profits. A declared social mission creates internal pressure to do more social good even when it may not be prudent, from a business point of view, to do so. Externally, cultural biases and political pressures can also work to inhibit earnings.

<u>Commitment to a social cause may compromise profits</u>. When one is committed to improving society, it is hard to say "enough." Social entrepreneurs may be tempted to plough potential profits back into good works or to take on unprofitable functions that would be more appropriate for nonprofits. Social commitments can weaken profits in many ways. Consider social ventures that employ or have as their customers disadvantaged populations. Serving those in the greatest need and doing it well can lead to decisions that have business costs. For example, Grameen Bank is world renowned for its micro-enterprise lending to Bangladesh's rural poor. In recent years, reported profits have declined about 85%, from $1.3 million in 1999 to just under $190,000 in 2001. Underlying this decline is a repayment problem, with reported loan-repayment rates falling well below the longtime, self-reported "over 95%" rate (Pearl & Phillips, 2001). Critics see this decline as raising serious questions about the model of a for-profit bank serving this market. While a 1998 flood and increased competition have contributed to these problems, another factor is the bank's commitment to its social mission. According to Grameen Founder Muhammed Yunus (2001),

We can raise our repayment rates to 100% instantaneously by a simple decision to write off all our overdue loans. We have more money in our loan-loss reserve ($67 million) than the present overdue loans. But we chose not to go that way. We want to do it the harder way – by improving the repayment situation and recovering the overdue amount. We do not want to abandon our borrowers/owners by disqualifying them to remain within the Grameen fold. We want them to change their life with Grameen. We don't want to push them away with their problems. We never think of walking away from them.

<u>For-profit social ventures often face strong cultural biases and political pressures against earning profits</u>. Our society seems to find something repulsive in the idea of someone profiting from "doing good." Indeed, it is almost a paradox of American culture that we applaud entrepreneurs who make their fortune with frivolous products, such as the "Pet Rock," but chastise those who would make the same profit (or even a generous salary) trying to make the world a better place. Without reliable and timely social performance measures, profits may be perceived as excessive, a situation that reinforces this cultural bias against profits in the social sector. Even where social impact is clear, many people still have a problem with entrepreneurs and investors in social ventures taking out profits when that money could be used to do more good. Social ventures tend to be held to a higher standard than other businesses.

Public skepticism can have dire consequences, especially if the government is the main paying customer. For instance, when Education Alternatives, Inc. was attempting to secure contracts to manage some of the Washington, DC public schools, public opposition helped derail the effort despite the initial support of the school superintendent Franklin L. Smith. The *Washington Post* quoted one women at a community forum, "Why, Dr. Smith, did we give you the job of running our schools if you decided to give up 15 schools to people who not only don't look like us but are just in it for the money? ... Our slave seller, Dr. Franklin Smith, is selling our education to the highest bidding rich white owner" (Horwitz, 1994). Criticisms such as these prompted Smith to table the school privatization proposal on the eve of the vote (Dees & Elias, 1995). Public suspicion and political pressures presented serious challenges for EAI, contributing to the company's ultimate failure to survive.

6. Strategies for Meeting the Challenges

The challenges facing for-profit social purpose ventures are significant. Thus, it is not surprising that conducting business for the public good "is an affection, indeed, not very common among merchants," as Adam Smith put it. Those who choose this path have their work cut out for them. However, there are strategies they can use to increase their chances of success. Our advice can be summed up in eight points.

6.1. Avoid Strategic Vagueness Regarding Mission

It almost goes without saying, but for-profit social entrepreneurs must be clear and open about their missions, including both social and economic objectives. Many social ventures are launched with rather vague missions and objectives. Vagueness allows each stakeholder to see what he or she wants in the venture. While this ambiguity may make it easier to attract resources, it is a recipe for conflict down the line. A clear mission that is communicated effectively helps screen prospective investors, employees, and customers, forming an implicit contract with them and encouraging positive self-selection. It also helps guide key strategic decisions.

6.2. Craft an Integrated and Compelling Venture Model

Social entrepreneurs must integrate a plausible social impact theory with a viable business model. The social impact theory should be open to scrutiny by those who are knowledgeable about the field in which the venture is operating, and the business model must make the case that this venture can have its intended social impact and make a sufficient profit at the same time. A strong business model will be built around opportunities where there is potential for significant congruence between social and economic value creation.[7] While this alignment is not easily achieved and requires rigorous analysis, for-profit social entrepreneurs may develop profitable strategies based on cost savings, serving neglected markets, or targeting socially oriented customers.

    Linking social cost savings to productivity improvements for customers. Reducing social costs can sometimes lead to lower economic costs or improved performance for potential customers. This effect was powerfully illustrated when corporations began looking for ways to be more environmentally friendly. Many of them found that being "green" could

---

7. When a more natural form of congruence is not available, social entrepreneurs can create linkages through various pricing mechanisms, service guarantees, and performance-based contracts. This approach can also help overcome fears of exploitation and profiteering. For example, a for-profit education company selling an innovative math curriculum could agree to be paid based on the number of students who achieve a certain proficiency level by the end of the program. A venture promoting a new, environmentally sustainable technology could offer a partial refund if the performance does not match or exceed the existing method of production. Of course, these types of policies are risky and may raise concerns for investors, but they can make customers more comfortable trying something new while explicitly linking income to social performance measures.

actually save them money by reducing materials and energy consumption as well as waste disposal costs (Hart, 1997). In 1995, a group of socially minded scientists formed Micell Technologies to capitalize on their CO_2-based technology that is designed to eliminate the need for toxic solvents without sacrificing precious water. Having had success applying its technology to the dry-cleaning industry, Micell continues to develop new applications and "prioritizes its development efforts by choosing CO_2-based applications where it can not only make an environmental impact, but where such processes provide a tangible performance benefit as well."[8] Merging a social purpose with cost and productivity considerations may help some social entrepreneurs identify viable new business opportunities.

Serving neglected labor or customer markets. Because of their social purpose, social entrepreneurs may be able to identify new markets, products, or services that have been overlooked by traditional businesses but provide opportunity for linking profit and social impact. For example, Voxiva is a voice and data solutions provider dedicated to bridging the digital divide by extending the reach of voicemail and automated business applications to anyone with access to a telephone. Operating in 20 Latin American companies, Voxiva provides solutions for health, finance, commercial, government, and small business operations that need to reach people who are beyond the reach of the Internet, do not have access to training, and may be illiterate. This business exemplifies the types of opportunities Stuart Hart and C.K. Prahalad (2002) describe as existing at "the bottom of the pyramid." According to Hart and Prahalad, the 4 billion people with less than $1500 annual income represent a multitrillion-dollar market. This market is "wide open for technological innovation" if companies will reexamine their current assumptions and adopt strategies focused on creating buying power, shaping aspirations, tailoring local solutions, and improving access for those currently left out of the global economy. As evidenced by Cooperative Home Care Associates' success employing low-income women as home health care professionals, similar arguments can be made with regard to neglected labor markets.

Targeting customers who value the kind of social impact you intend to create. If a for-profit social venture can develop a reputation for its social performance and deliver goods or services whose cost and quality are deemed on par with competitors, some customers may prefer their products due to their credible commitment to social impact. For example, though the success of Newman's Own all-natural food products certainly cannot be disassociated from Paul Newman, the fact that all of the profits are donated to charity likely attracts some customers when they are deciding amongst other comparably priced, similar quality, natural food products. This customer preference is not

---

8.   Retrieved from http://www.micell.com/default.asp?PID=2, 5/22/2002.

necessarily limited to retail products. For instance, demonstrated social commitment may be a deciding factor when school systems award charters, purchase curricula, or hire education management companies. CitySoft, an Internet applications provider committed to hiring its staff from inner city neighborhoods, provides another interesting example of this approach. In order to more effectively link its social mission to its business model, CitySoft recently decided to narrow its customer focus to "common interest enterprises," namely associations, foundations, non-profits, educational institutions, government agencies, and activist businesses. Notably, several of its clients are for-profit ventures mentioned elsewhere in this paper, including Shorebank Corporation, LearnNow, Stonyfield Farm, and Sustainable Jobs Fund. Of course, social entrepreneurs must be careful in assuming that customers will value their social commitments, especially if their business model requires charging a premium because of its social mission. Despite the opinion polls, most people still focus on cost, convenience, and quality. Relying on socially oriented customers may threaten the viability of the business by dramatically limiting its customer base. Moreover, even a credible social mission cannot compensate for other shortcomings in the customer value proposition.

6.3. Measure Performance Creatively and Test Assumptions Rigorously

Armed with a clear mission and venture model, the social entrepreneur should translate this information into quality standards, profit requirements, and performance measures. Since consumers and third-party payers cannot always be relied on to ensure quality, social purpose ventures must assume this burden themselves by committing to certain standards publicly and holding themselves accountable.[9] Likewise, they should determine minimum profit levels necessary for sustainability and track them, as well as social performance, closely.

While measuring social impact will always be a challenge, a social purpose venture should do its best to develop meaningful and credible measures. Social and economic goals can be broken down into specific, measurable process and outcome objectives, even if that means relying on indirect or leading indicators.[10] For example, an after-school program might have the following as two of its objectives for second quarter performance:

---

9. Setting clear standards should not be confused with providing the highest quality goods or services – after all, not every car is a Mercedes nor does every drug rehabilitation facility need to be a Betty Ford Clinic. Adding capacity and increasing access at lower quality and cost levels can be a valuable social service. See Dees and Anderson (2003).
10. For ideas about the right kinds of measures see Twersky, F., (2002) and Sawhill, J. & Williamson, D. (2000).

1000 students will have participated in our program at least three times a week, and by the end of the quarter, 75% of them will have increased their reading skills to the national average for fifth-graders. While the outcome measure is the true reflection of social impact, process measures are also important for understanding and tracking how the impact is being achieved. Similar metrics should be developed for financial progress. All of these targets and goals will provide a basis for managerial decision-making, communicating with stakeholders, and ongoing planning and development efforts related to product or service delivery.

An internal measurement system is critical for maintaining focus and guiding decision-making. However, social ventures should also periodically seek out independent, external evaluations. Few social ventures have the expertise in-house to conduct a rigorous and systematic evaluation of social impact. Outside evaluations can go beyond easy-to-track internal measures to examine cause and effect. They can also look across multiple organizations operating in the same arena to set benchmarks and detect larger patterns. Voluntarily submitting to this degree of scrutiny is risky, but the risk of receiving negative results is precisely what makes this process a valuable tool for both improving performance and enhancing credibility.

Finally, but perhaps most importantly, all of these measures and systems should be designed to test the underlying assumptions of the venture model, especially those that drive the links between social and economic performance. A social purpose venture should begin with a clear understanding of how both social and economic value will be created, but the strategy will likely need to be continuously refined and redefined as critical assumptions are put to the market test.[11]

6.4. Maintain Control in Sympathetic Hands

For profit social entrepreneurs need to pay particularly close attention to issues of ownership, investment, and control. Mary Houghton, the CEO of community development bank Shorebank Corporation, expressed her sentiment that given Shorebank's commitment to serving a public purpose, "ownership is really stewardship, not investment ownership" (Dees & Remey, 1994). The best stewards of the social and business purposes should own and control for-profit social ventures.

Before their venture models have proven to be sufficiently profitable, social entrepreneurs would be wise to target socially oriented investors. While

---

11. See McGrath and MacMillan (1995) to learn more about an approach to planning that begins with what you want to accomplish and then incorporates assumptions, milestones, testing, and refining as you learn.

this approach does limit the pool of potential capital providers, offsetting some of the potential benefits of the for-profit structure, it nonetheless ensures that its core investors share the dual commitment of social impact and profitability, providing some insulation from pure capital market pressures. While socially-oriented investors will usually expect a financial return, they are more likely to appreciate the complexity and experimental nature of the undertaking, to place equal or greater value on social performance, and to be patient while the venture tests and refines its model. Shorebank Corporation, for example, raised its initial funds from church groups, foundations, and socially committed individuals. According to one member of its founding management team, "One of the ways that we have achieved success was that our shareholders never wavered on why they invested. They invested because they believed that a business approach to development can work. They did not invest to get a market return" (Dees & Remey, 1994, p. 13). Of course, attracting socially oriented investors may not be a simple process, as different investors require different levels of financial return and liquidity, operate on different timetables, and place different value on the social return. However, targeting socially oriented investors should provide the venture with greater flexibility, especially in the early stages.

As the venture proves sufficiently profitable to attract more financially oriented investors, money can be raised from diverse sources, as long as *control* remains in the hands of those attuned to the mission. Some mechanisms for raising funds without threatening control include debt offerings, limited partnership shares, as well as forms of common and preferred stock with diluted or no voting rights. For instance, Shorebank has used private placements of preferred stock as well as common stock with no voting rights to raise capital while maintaining control in sympathetic hands. Teacher and worker cooperatives provide another example of using ownership as a means of holding a venture accountable to both social and financial performance.

Even some major corporations with strong social values maintain their social commitments by retaining control in the right hands. Levi Strauss & Company, which has a long history of social responsibility, became a public corporation in 1971 and included a statement of values in its prospectus. However, in 1985, family members repurchased the public stock, taking the company private to regain control and assure ongoing commitment to the company's core values. The company now uses high-yield debt instruments to raise capital. Other family-controlled firms with strong social values, such as The Timberland Company and The New York Times Corporation, have managed to tap into public equity markets without giving up enough control to jeopardize their social commitments. Timberland is well known for its strong values, progressive relationships with nonprofit organizations, and commitment to community service, social justice and environmental sustainability. The Swartz family, along with their trusts and foundations, own 55% of the stock and control 80% of the voting shares.[12] And despite the intense profit pressures on media companies in recent years, under the stewardship of the Salzburg family, *The New York Times* manages to attract top journalists, operate with high integrity, and deliver award-winning journalism to the public year after year. Of course, raising money from the public creates a fiduciary obligation to look out for the interests of those shareholders, but if the dual mission is clear in the public offering documents and *control* remains in sympathetic hands, the social purpose of the organization should be safe.

6.5. Invest Time and Energy in Creating a Committed Team

It is widely acknowledged that people are the most important factor in any new venture's success. As venture capitalist Ruthann Quindlen puts it, "People are to a business what location is to a restaurant" (2000, p. 33). This is doubly true for for-profit social ventures that must blend skills and values from two different fields. While attracting or building the necessary skills is critical, values should drive personnel decisions as much or more than skills. When trying to create a high-performance team, investing in selective hiring, appropriate performance-based compensation policies, training opportunities, and a balanced advisory board will significantly increase the chances of success (Pfeffer, 1998).

Considering the relatively small pool of candidates likely to already possess the desired combination of business and social sector skills, social ventures should cast a wide net when recruiting new team members. Finding the right team members can serve not only to build organizational skills, it can also send a signal to outsiders. Professionals with personal reputations or the right credentials can add credibility to the venture. When Chris Whittle hired Benno Schmidt, then the President of Yale University, to join him at Edison Schools, he was sending a signal that this was not to be just another profit-seeking business venture.

Though skills, credentials, and experience will be important, especially early on, ultimately selection should be based primarily on cultural fit, shared values, and a commitment to pursuing social impact via business methods. Successful screening on these factors depends not only on reviewing a large pool of applicants, but also on engaging in a lengthy hiring process that involves multiple interactions with a wide variety of existing employees and key stakeholders. This process requires some patience and a willingness to

---

12. Retrieved from http://www.hoovers.com/co/capsule/0/0,2163,12390,00.html, accessed 05/24/02.

invest time and money into recruiting, and it may mean growing at a slower rate. It may also require investing in training opportunities to develop needed skills. Whether developed in-house or provided by outside contractors, both hard skills and soft-skills training may help bridge some of the cultural and practical differences that will inevitably be present if hiring from a diversity of backgrounds and experiences in both the business and social sectors. In addition to training, once credible measurement systems are in place, social entrepreneurs should also explore the creation of bonus plans that are tied both to profit and social value objectives. It may even be useful to create financial and other incentives that reward innovative approaches to both social and business problems, especially those that help the organization align the dual objectives more closely.

Beyond appropriate hiring, compensating, and training of the venture team, it can be quite helpful to establish an advisory board with representatives from a wide range of experience, including careers in business, entrepreneurship, nonprofit organizations, and the public sector. For example, Voxiva's advisory board consists of social entrepreneurs with nonprofit and government backgrounds, experts in technology and the digital divide, a financial expert with experience related to emerging markets, and an attorney with expertise in international relations. This composition signals to staff that both financial and social goals are paramount, provides them with role models from different arenas, and helps to ensure that the organization's dual objective is present from the top to the bottom of the organization.

6.6. Anticipate Resistance and Develop a Strategy for Dealing with It

For-profit social entrepreneurs will likely encounter resistance and distrust. They need to anticipate potential sources of concern and develop a strategy for dealing with them. Politics are important to any new venture. However, given their controversial character, politics are potentially particularly important for for-profit social ventures. These ventures may expect to be held to different standards than other for-profit companies.

For-profit social ventures may head off some resistance by operating transparently, communicating effectively, avoiding excess, and acting as good corporate citizens. Sharing the venture's mission, its social impact theory, its business model, and its performance information actively and openly can reduce reasons for distrust. Giving key stakeholders a voice through regular interaction or even advisory board membership can also allay concerns. Moreover, like their nonprofit counterparts, social entrepreneurs would be politically wise to avoid what may be perceived as excesses in compensation, personal expenditures, office environments, and corporate perks. Additionally, contributing some portion of profits to charitable causes and participating in community service activities can help build goodwill and overcome public resistance. The founders of 4charity.com, an Internet applications company that serves the social sector, even set aside a substantial portion of their founding stock for nonprofit organizations.

Even with transparency, openness, and modest salaries and perks, social ventures may meet with formidable resistance. Collaborating with trusted nonprofit partners might also help a venture overcome both customer and public distrust. For example, the charter school firm LearnNow partners with local groups and organizations that have strong ties to the communities where LearnNow operates schools. These partnerships provide LearnNow with access to valuable local knowledge and expertise, while also giving the communities a voice in the educational process and affording the opportunity to build a trusting relationship between the company and the communities they serve.

In general, social entrepreneurs should assess the political environments in which they are operating and develop an appropriate strategic response. This process can begin with identifying key players. Who are potential critics or enemies? Who is likely to feel threatened? Whose cooperation is necessary for success? Once social entrepreneurs have identified important parties and assessed their motivations, they can explore options for dealing with potential resistance by co-opting the critics, building rapport with them, or forming coalitions to overcome them (MacMillan, 1992).

6.7. Develop a Brand Reputation for Quality and Performance

Over the long haul, it can be very helpful to develop a brand reputation that signals serious commitment to both social impact and business discipline. As a venture grows, the brand serves as the carrier of the venture's reputation, representing a track record as well as a set of demonstrated values. Brand credibility can also be borrowed from and shared with other organizations. For-profit social ventures may find that forming strategic alliances with like-minded ventures could help them build credibility, signal their commitment to quality and social value, and access new customers. For example, Stonyfield Farm, producer of organic ice cream and yogurt, has formal relationships with other "earth-friendly" partners, including Newman's Own, Recycline, and others. For participating companies, these alliances serve as endorsements of each other's environmental practices and commitment, allowing each of them to build on the others' brands and consumer trust while also gaining exposure to their environmentally oriented customer bases.

6.8. Recognize the Limits of What Can Be Done For-Profit and Use Nonprofit
Partners or Affiliates to Provide Complementary Services

Strategic collaboration with nonprofits may help for-profit social ventures
ensure profitability without sacrificing social performance. Creating social
benefit is a complex process. When pursuing social impact, there are often
complementary activities that would contribute to a social venture's success
but cannot be done profitably. In these cases, it helps to have a nonprofit
partner or to be operating in a hybrid organization that includes a nonprofit
affiliate. Indeed, both Grameen Bank and Shorebank Corporation have
operated as hybrid organizations with nonprofit affiliates for many years. More
recently, soon after its launch, the leaders of CitySoft, a web development and
management firm committed to hiring predominantly lower-income urban
adults, realized that existing training programs were not effectively preparing
urban adults for success in high tech careers. Thus, CitySoft spun-off a
nonprofit called CitySkills to partner with training organizations and
employers to create the necessary infrastructure and "labor pipelines" for
recruiting, training, and placing inner-city residents in upwardly mobile
information technology jobs. The Sustainable Jobs Fund (SJF), a for-profit
community development venture capital fund that invested in City Soft and
other companies, followed the same path, recently establishing the Sustainable
Jobs Development Corporation, a nonprofit that provides additional technical
and community development assistance to SJF's prospective and portfolio
companies. Providing this service under the for-profit fund would potentially
limit returns to investors. However, the provision of these services is important
to achieving the kind of economic and social impact that SJF set out to create.
As these examples illustrate, hybrid organizational structures and partnerships
with nonprofits may allow a social venture to better serve its economic and
social goals by ensuring the provision of complementary activities by
organizations that are better positioned to subsidize these activities through
philanthropic support.

7. Concluding Thoughts

It may be feasible to marry a social purpose to a for-profit structure, but it is
not easy. Even ventures such as Shorebank Corporation and Grameen Bank,
which have withstood the test of time and received much acclaim, have
encountered major challenges. Shorebank has not generated market rates of
return for its investors (Esty, 1995). Other than one small dividend, its
common stock holders did not have liquidity for over twenty years. Not
surprisingly, the model has not spread very rapidly. Grameen spread rapidly in
Bangladesh and has inspired similar programs worldwide, but its profitability

has been overshadowed by its reliance on below-market rate capital. Duplicating Grameen's profitability has proven to be much more difficult than duplicating its approach to lending. And Grameen has recently encountered serious questions about its financial performance (Pearl & Phillips, 2001). It may have become a victim of its own success, as many mircocredit lenders have entered the market and created new competitive pressures that may limit Grameen's growth and reduce its profitability. And while some people may question whether Edison Schools is truly a social purpose venture, the company's failure to turn a profit and its current financial struggles raise serious questions about the sustainability and scalability of certain types of for-profit social ventures.

In fact, in many cases, it may be easier to achieve the same or greater social impact as a nonprofit. Many creative and entrepreneurial social ventures have been successfully launched as nonprofits. For example, North Carolina's Self Help Credit Union has a mission similar to Shorebank's but is incorporated as a nonprofit, with both nonprofit and for-profit subsidiaries. In 2000, Self Help's pre-tax income of $9.8 million more than quadrupled Shorebank's $2.3 million. We do not mean to be critical of Shorebank or to argue that SelfHelp has a better model. Rather, we merely want to demonstrate that profitability, business discipline, and an entrepreneurial spirit are not restricted to for-profit organizations. Thus, before adopting a for-profit structure, we urge social entrepreneurs to analyze which approach is best. While the nonprofit structure does impose some constraints on raising capital and distributing profits, many for-profit social ventures are also limited in their ability to take full advantage of the capital markets and produce significant profits and returns. And while some nonprofit cultures and norms are certainly not conducive to these types of ventures, strong and visionary leaders can overcome these biases. Additionally, nonprofit organizations do offer some benefits of their own, including access to philanthropic resources (cash, in-kind, and volunteers) and less inherent skepticism of their motives. We do not want to downplay the potential benefits of the for-profit firm, but we do encourage social entrepreneurs to make a well-informed, strategic decision regarding which structure will best serve their objectives.

If the nonprofit alternative is not appealing, social entrepreneurs should contemplate the benefits, challenges, and strategies outlined here and follow Amar Bhide's (1995) advice to complement "perseverance and tenacity" with "flexibility and a willingness to learn." We recommend for-profit social entrepreneurs be clear and perseverant about their social and economic objectives, but flexible about the strategies they will employ for achieving them. As long as they are clear about their social and economic goals, measure their performance rigorously, maintain control of the venture in the hands of the best stewards, and invest in hiring and developing the right people, for-profit social entrepreneurs should have the time and opportunity to identify where economic and social value can and cannot be aligned successfully, what strategies are most effective for overcoming criticism and political adversaries, and what complementary activities might best be accomplished by a nonprofit partner. Thus, if social entrepreneurs remain tenacious regarding their overarching social and economic ambitions, they can be flexible and adapt their strategies for achieving their objectives as they learn.

References

Arrow, K. (1973). "Social Responsibility and Economic Efficiency". *Public Policy, 21*, 303-317.

Baumol, W. (1991). *Perfect Markets and Easy Virtue*. Cambridge, MA: Basil Blackwell.

Bhide, A. (1994). "How Entrepreneurs Craft Strategies That Work". *Harvard Business Review*, March-April, 150-161.

Dees, J. G. & Anderson, B. B. (2003). "Sector Bending: Blurring the Lines between Nonprofit and For-Profit". *Society (Social Sciences and Modern Society), 40* (4), 16-27.

Dees. J.G. & Anderson, B. (2001). "New Schools (A) and (B)," Stanford Business School, SI-07A and SI-07B.

Dees, J. G. & Elias, J. (1995). "Education Alternatives, Inc." Harvard Business School Publishing, 9-395-106.

Dees, J.G. & Remey, C.C. (1994). "Shorebank Corporation", Harvard Business School Publishing, 9-393-096.

Emerson, J. (2000). "The Nature of Returns: A Social Capital Markets Inquiry into Elements of Investment and The Blended Value Proposition." Harvard Business School, Social Enterprise Series No. 17, available for download at http://www.hbs.edu/socialenterprise/download/.

Esty, B.C. (1995). "South Shore Bank: Is it the Model of Success for Community Development Banks?". *Psychology & Marketing, 12*, 8, 789-819.

Flannery, D. & Deiglmeier, K. (1999). "Managing the Social Purpose Enterprise", *The REDF Box Set – Volume 1* (pp. 11-18), available at http://www.redf.org/pub_boxset.htm

Friedman, M. (1962). *Capitalism and Freedom*. Chicago: University of Chicago Press.

Grossman, A., Austin, J., Hart, M. & Peyus, S. I. (1999). "Explore, Inc.", Harvard Business School Publishing, 9-300-011.

Haberman, J. (2001). "Executive Jobs in For-Profit Education: Risk or Opportunity?" *The Chronicle of Higher Education*, January 12, retrieved May 17, 2002 from http://chronicle.com/jobs/2001/01/2001011202c.htm.

Hansmann, H. (1980). "The Role of Nonprofit Enterprise". *Yale Law Journal, 89*, 835-901.

Hansmann, H. (1996). "The Changing Roles of Public, Private, and Nonprofit Enterprise in Education, Health Care, and Other Human Services". In V.R. Fuchs, Victor (Ed.), *Individual and Social Responsibility: Child Care, Education, Medical Care, and Long-Term Care in America*. Chicago: University of Chicago Press.

Hart, S.L. (1997). "Beyond Greening: Strategies for a Sustainable World". *Harvard Business Review*, January-February, 66-76.

Horwitz, S. (1994). "A public defeat on privatization: DC superintendent's plan unravels amid charges of racism". *Washington Post*, March 5, B1.

MacMillan, I. C. (1992). "The Politics of New Venture Management". In *The Entrepreneurial Venture: Readings Selected by William A. Shalman and Howard H. Stevenson* (pp. 160-168). Boston: Harvard Business School Press.

McGrath, R.G. & MacMillan, I.C. (1995). "Discovery-Driven Planning". *Harvard Business Review*, July-August, 4-12.

Pearl, D. & Phillips, M. (2001). "Grameen Bank, Which Pioneered Loans For the Poor, Has Hit a Repayment Snag". *Wall Street Journal*, November 27, retrieved from http://www.wsj.com, 5/28/2002.

Pfeffer, J. (1998) "Seven Practices of Successful Organizations". *California Management Review, 40*, 2, 96-124.

Quindlen, R. (2000). *Confessions of a Venture Capitalist: Inside the High Stakes World of Start-Up Financing*. New York: Warner Books.

Porter, M. E. (1985). *Competitive Advantage: Creating and Sustaining Superior Performance*. New York: The Free Press.

Prahalad, C.K. & Hart, S. L. (2002). "The Fortune at the Bottom of the Pyramid". *strategy+business*, First Quarter, 54-67.

Rangan, V. K., Karem, S., & Sandberg, S. K. (1996) "Do Better at Doing Good". *Harvard Business Review*, May-June, 4-11.

Ryan, W. P., (1999) "The New Landscape for Nonprofits," *Harvard Business Review*, January-February, 127-136.

Sawhill, J. & Williamson, D. (2000) "Measuring What Matters in Nonprofits", *McKinsey Quarterly*, *2*, 98-107.

Smith, A. (1776). *An Inquiry into the Nature and Causes of the Wealth of Nations*, reprinted by University of Chicago Press: Chicago, 1976.

Twersky, F. (2002). "Performance Information That Really Performs". In Dees, J.G., Emerson, J. & Economy, P. (Eds.) *Strategic Tools for Social Entrepreneurs: Enhancing the Performance of Your Enterprising Nonprofit* (pp. 161-188). New York: John Wiley & Sons.

Welles, E.O. (1998). "Ben's Big Flop". *Inc.*, *20*, 12, 40-57.

Yunus, M. (2001) Letter to the Editor, *Wall Street Journal*, December 12, retrieved from http://www.grameen-info.org/wallstreetjournal/LetterToWSJEditor.html, 5/28/2002.

Social Entrepreneurship edited by Marilyn L. Kourilsky and William B. Walstad
© *2003, Senate Hall Academic Publishing.*

3. Social Capital, Social Entrepreneurship and Entrepreneurship Education

Calvin A. Kent and Lorraine P. Anderson
Marshall University

Abstract. This paper integrates the concepts of "social capital" and "social entrepreneurship" into the study of entrepreneurship. It contends that understanding the role that social organizations play in the process of innovation is essential to fully understand how ideas become new ventures. Moreover the paper makes the case that solving the social problems of the day requires the same type of risk taking and innovative thinking which characterized the production of new products and services. It calls attention to the significant volume of research which illustrates how the formation of social capital is essential for economic growth and provides the framework in which entrepreneurship can take place. Closing the paper is a discussion of how the concepts of "social capital" and "social entrepreneurship" should be integrated into the entrepreneurship curriculum at all levels of instruction.

Keywords: entrepreneurship, entrepreneurship education, social capital, social entrepreneurship, economic growth, innovation and investment.

1. Introduction

Entrepreneurship is about change and transformation. Its about new ideas and how they come to be useful products, technologies and services. Its about new ventures and how they grow. In the public mind it is often associated as being about new technology. Such associations are unfortunate. Not because they are entirely wrong, but because they are too restricting.

Studying change and innovation should not be limited to business or technology. Innovation is more than new products and processes for production. Entrepreneurship should encompass all of societies interactions, not just those bounded by the market. The focus of this paper is on a form of entrepreneurship which has existed from the beginning, but is only recently becoming a matter of inquiry. It concerns the social interactions of people and solving the issues which result from that interaction. That interaction can take place on may levels; the firm, a non-profit organization, a government or even a nation.

It has been labeled as "social entrepreneurship" and its study pushes forward the scope of entrepreneurship research. At the heart of this social entrepreneurship is the creation of "social capital". It is the purpose of this paper to explore the concept of social capital and its relationship to social entrepreneurship and how the concept is being taught in business related courses at the pre-college and collegiate level. This paper concludes with a call for action.

Unfortunately the study of entrepreneurship in many instances has become focused on technology and the ventures which produce it. In light of the recent rash of dot.com failures, it should be abundantly clear that having even the most advanced technology does not guarantee entrepreneurial success in today's global economy. This is a world of rapid change driven by technological advancements. It is easy to understand why entrepreneurs, investors and those who educate them are seduced into the belief that they must have the newest toys on the market. Tom Peters says to focus on creating a company that will "wow" the customer, and many of today's products do indeed "wow" us. But technology alone will not lead a company to become a leader. Nor will it provide a better society characterized by harmony and progress. Success in business and society requires relationship-based organizations, "social communities", based on trust, commitment, and mission.

Technology, entrepreneurship and these social communities are compatible, but they must be kept in perspective. To remain competitive, an institution must keep up with technological advancements. But technology, even the best, will take any organization only half as far as it needs to go. The people in organizations, both business and social, take them all the way to success. The mission of entrepreneurs and entrepreneurship educators, is to tap into the energy and insights of the workforce and our graduates and let them carry economic advancement to new heights. But this provides only a limited view of the potential for change which entrepreneurship can bring. Entrepreneurs can be the change agents for creating social as well as material progress. Creating the social capital which can knit the frayed structure of society also requires the same risk taking and innovation. Building better products and providing better services is not all entrepreneurs can accomplish. But how many entrepreneurs know how to create social capital? How many curriculums, either in pre-collegiate or collegiate entrepreneurship, can say that skill is imparted to their students?

2. The Concept of Social Capital

This paper has as its focus one aspect of social entrepreneurship, the creation of social capital. There is a growing recognition among scholars and observers of the "new economy" that one element has not changed. What Coleman and others call "social capital" remains the foundation of economic progress. Cohen and Prusak in their recent study find social capital consisting of, "...the stock of active connections among people, the trust, mutual understanding and shared values and behaviors that bind the members of human networks and communities and make cooperative action possible" (p. 4). They list the following characteristics of social capital: high levels of trust, robust personal networks, vibrant communities, shared understandings and equity participation in decision making.

The Saquaro Seminar developed a national survey of social capital community benchmarks. This association of scholars and thinkers surveyed 30,000 respondents in 40 communities across 29 states. Their survey was designed "to measure the amount of social capital in various communities" as well as the distribution of social capital within a community (p. 6). The survey assessed people's responses to questions concerning 11 facets of social capital: social trust, interracial trust, diversity of friendships, political participation, political protest, civic leadership, associational involvement, informal socializing, giving and volunteering, faith-based engagement and equality of civic engagement. The results indicated that a sense of community is a much stronger predictor of personal happiness and the perceived quality of life in a geographical area than either income or educational level.

Voices of dissent to the value of social capital to economic growth and entrepreneurship are present. Florida, based on his own research and that of others, concluded that communities with demonstrated high levels of social capital did not necessarily experience faster economic growth than others. He felt the statistical studies supporting the value of social capital in high growth communities failed to consider other factors that may have been more important in explaining their high growth rates. Further, he found a dark side to social capital. Individuals, particularly ethnic minorities, were often excluded from the social communities that resulted from the formation of social capital.

3. Dimensions of Social Capital

The creation of social capital has both an internal and external dimension. Internally the creation of social capital increases the effectiveness of the firm or other organization. This is accomplished by establishing an environment where workers, particularly knowledge workers, can have the space, time and support to create. Most discussion of social capital has been concerned with this internal aspect.

The external aspects of social capital are only in the infant stage of inquiry. Since external social capital encompasses sociological and political issues as well as economic, it begs for an interdisciplinary approach. The creation of external social capital by social entrepreneurs is the way to increase the effectiveness of social institutions with the anticipated result, not of greater profits, but of expanded social harmony.

4. Economics and Social Capital

Beginning with Putnam's landmark work *Bowling Alone*, the economic value of social capital has been repeatedly demonstrated. His work details the problems associated with the decline of American social capital. Studies for the World Bank compiled by Narayan, suggest that differences in regional economic growth may be explained primarily because many of the underdeveloped lands lack even basic social capital. Russia, Argentina and most of Africa can be given as examples of areas rich in natural resources but almost entirely bereft of social capital. Corruption, revolution and tribal warfare rather than economic advancement characterize these places. Woolcock has suggested a multi-disciplinary approach to the study of social capital may lead to finding answers to the most pressing economic and social issues of our time.

Although almost totally absent from most economics texts, the reasons why social capital is pivotal in the process of economic growth should be understood by any student of the "dismal science". Decades ago, Coase introduced the concept of "transaction costs" for which he was to win the Nobel Prize in Economics. He contended that businesses, as well as entire economies, which become more specialized and interdependent must engage in a widening spiral of relationships or transactions. These transactions are expensive in terms of resource use, time, money and effort. Reducing the number and difficulty of these transactions increased economic efficiency. The greater the supply of social capital the easier it is to work out transactions and lower production costs. That is why Cohen and Prusak can confidently assert, "...social capital generates economic returns" (p. 10).

It is not surprising that economists with their preoccupation with arcane economic modeling have missed the importance of social capital. But they should not have. The first economist, Adam Smith, made it clear that economic life and social life, including culture, habits, and mores, can not be separated. Modern neo-classical economics divorces individual behavior and the action of firms from the social setting. All individuals act in their "self interest" maximizing their utility. Firms are "profit maximizers" concerned primarily with the bottom line and return to shareholders. Fukuyama debunks these concepts in his investigation and concludes, "The greatest economic efficiency was not necessarily achieved by rational self-interested utility maximizing individuals, but, rather, by groups of individuals who, because of a preexisting moral community, are able to work together effectively" (p. 21).

5. Thoughts from the Left

While conservative, free market advocates may be loth to confess it, the left may have found an important truth about the role of labor in the new, knowledge based economy. At the start of her book Kelly concludes, "For many companies knowledge is the new source of competitive advantage" (p. 6). Knowledge resides with employees, including managers, who are the real wealth creators.

For some this may sound like a revival of Karl Marx's "labor theory of value" in which all returns from productive enterprise are to be allocated to labor. Capital can be dismissed from the economic equation as it is nothing more than the embodiment of the past labor which created it. For those who may have forgotten his words, "...only human sweat and skill is the true source of all value". Kelly illustrates her point by reference to the "St. Luke's maneuver" where the employees of a London "knowledge" based public relations company resisted a hostile merger by quitting in mass. By that action the value of the company to the acquiring firm evaporated.

6. Social Capital and Trust

Social capital depends foremost on trust. As Locke wrote, "Trust is like the air we breathe; it is basic to all human activities" (p. 110). The clearest expression is found in Fukuyama after an exhaustive study of economic history noted, "...the most important lesson we can learn from an examination of economic life is that a nation's well being, as well as its ability to compete, is conditioned by a single, pervasive cultural characteristic: the level of trust inherent in the society" (p. 7).

In its most basic understanding, trust comes from human interaction. People who know each other and have favorable interactions can depend on the other. Trust can then replace rules and regulations as guides for human behavior. Informal personal relationships replace complex commandments. Transaction costs are reduced in an organization, or even a nation, where people trust each other.

7. Trust and Technology

What differentiates the "new economy" from the old is the increased speed with which new technology is developed and expected to be implemented. Technology has always created change and disruption with the counterparts of fear and dislocation. In other words, technology is the harbinger of what Duck calls the "change monster." Based on her extensive investigations and work with many leading firms, she feels the pace of economic growth in the new economy is slowed by the resistance to the changes which technology brings. After all it is people who create, implement and adapt the new technology. To the extent they fear the changes, real or imagined, which may result, technological advance is inhibited. As she finds, "...the emotional aspects of change are not just important, they are vital" (p. 9).

In a most provocative book Brown and Duguid review the "social context for technology." They see a world in which technology is surging ahead but society is lagging behind. To them the greatest problem faced by those who make business decisions today is overestimating the impact of technology and underestimating the impact of human needs. They contend that most technology is developed with the assumption that people work in isolation, with little need for "face to face" contact, and that technology will work as designed. None of these are correct. Workers must be able to own, control and modify the technology. For this to happen people must interact sharing insights, failures and improvisations.

Brown and Duguid see a sharp distinction between information and knowledge and contend that current emphasis on the "information economy" be replaced with stress on the role of knowledge. Information is basically sterile and can easily be transferred, but knowledge – how to use information – requires understanding the data, assimilating it and becoming committed to applying it in new and creative ways. As they see it, society is "drowning in information" and knowledge is the only "lifeboat" available.

Though we live in a society addicted to the pursuit of speed and technological advancements, this does not preclude the development of relationship-based organizations. It is people who make change happen. Marshall writes, "Not only are speed and trust compatible, but there can be no sustained speed at work without trust" (p. 103). He believes that we must change traditional organizations to those that value principle over power and people over process and technique. All business including those which are entrepreneurial need to strengthen their relationships with our employees, suppliers, and even our competitors. "Speed happens when people trust each other" (p. 103).

Employees are becoming as mobile as money. Technology has assured that labor, particularly knowledge workers, are not place bound. Most knowledge work can be accomplished virtually anywhere. The Internet has assured that. As a result human capital and the social capital which supports it must be viewed differently by educators than has been past practice

The historian Adas provides a negative view of technological change as the most often cited reason for economic advance. While concluding that technology has been the basis for rising living standards at all places and all times in world history, he feels that the almost exclusive focus on physical technology has led to a misunderstanding of the real forces which lie behind continuous improvement. While one does not have to accept his obvious dislike for what he views as the dehumanization which results from an overemphasis on the role of technology, his view that culture and the evolution of human relationships have been the causes for the discovery, acceptance and widespread dispersion of technology is persuasive. Without social capital technological progress would not have happened at the speed with which it is transpiring or been so quickly or broadly disseminated.

8. Social Capital and Entrepreneurship

There is a strong relationship between technological innovation and trust which may not be obvious. The key to learning is being a member of a "social community" which shares its insights and practices. The stronger that community the greater the level of trust that is likely to develop. This trust encourages risk taking as it reduces the possibility and consequences of failure. As risk taking becomes the norm, the yield is innovation.

This explains why so many recent studies of entrepreneurial firms have found a high correlation between trust and other forms of social capital and organizational success (Collins and Collins, O'Reilly and Pfeffner, Stewart). Goshal and Barlett remark, "On the organizational trapeze, individuals will take the entrepreneurial leap only if they believe there will be a strong and supportive pair of hands at the other end to catch them" (p. 93).

Often referred to as the "soft skills" of management, tried and true values are what can take an organization from being ordinary to extraordinary. Technology can dazzle investors and mesmerize entrepreneurs, but when the layers of today's truly successfully entrepreneurial companies are peeled back to their essentials, there is found an emphasis on people.

To cite but one example from many of a firm which developed internal social capital. When Dave Longaberger died in 1999 he left behind a legacy. Under his leadership, Longaberger Basket grew from 350 employees and $8 million in sales in 1984 to over 8,000 employees and $1 billion in sales in 2000. Many would consider Longaberger a self-taught entrepreneur, yet he stated that everything he knew about business, he learned from his mom and dad. Longaberger said, "I don't care what business you're in, your success will ultimately depend on the relationships you build with people"(p. xv). Successful businesses are built on trust between company and customer, employer and employee, and employees and their colleagues. Employers must prove themselves to their people, day in and day out. Longaberger cautioned to never assume that employees will automatically trust us because we hand them paychecks. "You have to earn their trust. And, once you have it, you have to keep earning it" (p. 42). The same is true for any organization. Trust, once compromised, is difficult to regain.

Successful entrepreneurs must listen to employees and give them the freedom to make changes they believe will benefit the company. In the business world, Longaberger proved that listening to employees and trusting them to keep the company's best interests at heart makes good sense. Longaberger was selected as a co-winner of the 2001 RIT/USA Today Quality Cup in manufacturing because the company trusted its employees.

For example, three basket weavers on the shop floor recognized that each weaver was not getting the correct material to make the basket design assigned to him or her, leading to constant, time-consuming trading of raw materials and inefficient hoarding. Morale started to suffer. When the three weavers set out to study the problem, they were given top support by management and encouragement from the CEO. On a paid sabbatical from weaving, the team obtained training in flow charting, cause-and-effect analysis and problem solving. The changes they recommended have resulted in a savings of $3 million per year, and that number is rising.

The management team at Longaberger took their founder's and social words of wisdom to heart. They rely, day in and day out, on the old values of trust and commitment as they work toward developing strong relationships and social capital for the betterment of the company.

9. Leadership and Social Capital

Whether an individual is at the helm of a for-profit organization like Longaberger or a non-profit organization, those interested in creating social capital should develop the capacity to lead as well as manage. Harvard's John Kotter introduced the difference between management and leadership in his book, *Leading Change.* Kotter suggests the following distinction: management skills produce a degree of predictability and order that has the potential to consistently produce short-term results expected by stakeholders.

- Planning and Budgeting

- Controlling and Problem Solving

- Organizing and Staffing

By way of comparison leadership skills produce change, often to a dramatic degree and have the potential to produce extremely useful change that stakeholders want.

- Establishing direction

- Aligning people

- Motivating and Inspiring (p. 26)

Management skills tend to yield consistent results or status quo. Leadership skills require the ability to develop a vision for the future and then motivate others to work toward the accomplishment of that goal.

Best-selling author Ken Blanchard has devoted the last 15 years of his career to helping managers become better leaders. Although neither Kotter or Blanchard used the term social capital, both management consultants stress the importance of trust, communication skills, and strong relationships in any organization as necessary for creating change and innovation. Blanchard wrote, "Leadership is not something you do *to* people, but something you do *with* people" (p. 140). A leader must understand that effective leadership is a two-way relationship. Communication and trust must flow between the manager and the employees. This positive relationship does not develop in a vacuum or without effort. Leaders must take the responsibility themselves for making their relationships with their employees work. There is not a one-size-fits-all approach to achieve this trust.

Robert Greenleaf introduced the concept of "servant leadership" to the business world. He encouraged leaders to think of themselves as working for their employees in term of supporting whatever they need, i.e. materials, training, encouragement, rewards, or recognition to get the job done. This outstanding concept has been embraced by many, but Blanchard suggests that servant leadership is more about character than style. Too often entrepreneurs when they manage race to use a new management technique. Workers become confused, and perhaps a little jaded for they recognize technique over sincerity every time. Leaders don't all have to manage or lead the same way, but they do need to recognize that true leadership is rooted in mutual trust.

Blanchard states, "Real communication happens when people feel safe" (p. 68). This point was reinforced by DeMarco who feels that many organizations, both non-profit and profit making, exist in a "culture of fear". Fear of failure to met deadlines, make budget, hit sales targets, or to have new products, processes or policies work as intended. According to both authors regardless of age, gender or race, leaders need to be honest with their employees. Praise them for their accomplishments, no matter how small. Give honest feedback when someone is headed down the wrong path or their work is not up to par. This honesty will be respected and will build a trusting relationship. Most important will be cutting your subordinates some "slack" so they will have time to create and to try without fear of failure..

With most entrepreneur managers, the problem that arises is not due to malice or a lack of caring, but to benign neglect. Entrepreneur leaders need to actively work toward building social capital with those whom they work with in their organizations. People today seem to be so busy doing things that are urgent, but not important. Reports and paperwork demand our time, but at what cost? For DeMarco the cost is loss of innovation.

What leadership research teaches entrepreneurs is to gives as much attention to their co-workers as they do to the new idea. Listen to what they are saying. Find out what motivates them and verbalize your thoughts and feelings. Entrepreneurs who seek to lead, should not assume that their subordinates know what they think. Tell them. As Blanchard so eloquently put it, "Good thoughts in your head not delivered mean squat" (p. 52).

The words "entrepreneurship" and "leadership" do not bring to mind images of reports or balance sheets. Leadership implies a group of people moving toward the goal that unites them. Too much time spent on the inanimate assets of a company does not build social capital. Balance is the key. While the body of research on leadership has not yet become directly concerned with social capital or social entrepreneurship, the principles are directly applicable to bring change either within an organization or the larger society. The quest is for new ideas that solve social problems rather than effectiveness in delivery or production of goods and services.

Certainly the servant leader concept can be broadened to include service to a wider community than just those within the immediate organization itself. Concern for others should motivate entrepreneurs to seek a better society not just a more efficient firm. An effective entrepreneur leader understands that through strong relationships build on trust, great accomplishments follow naturally.

The success of Pam Curry and the Center for Economic Options in West Virginia is an example. In 2001, she and her organization were recognized with the Presidential Award for Excellence in Microenterprise Development for Program Innovation. As she reports for nearly 20 years her organization has, "created innovative ways to help entrepreneurs – especially those in rural areas – become engaged in the economy and experience economic self-reliance" (p. 7). Most of these are tiny operations having fewer than five employees with low start-up and capital needs. Many of theses are home based and make use of forest and farm products. As Curry summed the Center's philosophy, "Rural microenterprises depend on an unspoiled wilderness, clean water and a healthy environment.... (The Center) believes that developing sustainable enterprises will not only decrease the number of household falling below the poverty line and promote local control and economic stability, but also will increase the value placed on sustaining West Virginia's natural resources" (p. 7).

Many of these enterprises assisted by the Center have become profitable companies. The Center has a large and profitable outlet store in a major mall and an active internet site. None of this would have happened if Curry had not been willing to lead. Since most of her co-workers are volunteers or part-time, the skills of entrepreneur leader have been repeatedly employed in Curry's achievements.

10. Accounting for Social Capital

The curriculum of most business programs, including those who claim to emphasize entrepreneurship, have not paid sufficient attention to social capital. To cite one example. Accounting is in deep difficulty. There is a phenomenal and growing gap between reality and accounting theory and practice. In the case of Enron, the failure of either the Securities and Exchange Commission or the American Institute of CPA's to understand or adapt to the mega-changes in the way companies financed themselves left gaping loopholes in accounting standards. These oversights allowed practices, while clearly unethical, which may not technically be illegal. According to Smith "off-book" entities, capitalization of current costs, changes in depreciation accounts and the treatment of buy/sell contracts in conventional accounting illustrate this failure.

But an even more subtle and difficult problem exists for accountants and finance professionals: How does one account for human and social capital? Shutt has called attention to the, "...transformation in the nature of the asset base of capitalist enterprises" (p. 102). For a rapidly expanding number of firms their assets are human "software" of technical knowhow, managerial expertise, communication skills and network relationships. These intangible items are not to be found as specific assets on the corporation's books.

The best accounting can do now is to classify the contribution of these to the companies value as "good will" or "intangibles", which is nothing more than the difference between the acquiring price of the firm and the net value of depreciated physical capital. Intangibles include more than social capital. Brand names, patents, customer base, reputation for service and/or quality are also included. In his book Handy sums the dilemma by noting that the value of knowledge companies is due to the presence of key individuals with outstanding capabilities.

These intangibles cannot be classified as fixed assets upon which the accountant can place a predictable value. This human capital may leave the firm migrating elsewhere leaving the original firm with limited capacity to compete. Shutt is correct when he notes, "...given the impact of intangible factors in extending the scope for subjective valuation of companies... there are stronger grounds than ever for treating company financial statements with suspicion" (p. 103).

The tax codes of most industrialized nations continue this neglect. While there are tax credits and accelerated depreciation for tangible physical capital such as buildings and machinery, social capital does not receive such favorable treatment.   Section 197 of the IRS Code delineates the treatment of "intangibles". It provides for amortization of these over a 15 year period in most instances. As Pope, Anderson and Kramer found, Section 197 applied only to intangible assets that were *acquired*. Section 197 did not apply to an intangible asset that was internally created by the firm.

Put simply, any accretion to human or social capital which the firm creates receives no positive tax treatment unless that firm is sold. In this case it becomes the "good will" portion of the selling price and the buyer does receive a tax concession. But investment in social capital on a continuing basis receives no such reward. Given this favorable tax environment, it is small wonder physical capital dominates when investment considerations are made. Giving credit for investment in social capital would encourage its further formation.

11. From Social Capital to Social Entrepreneurship

Social capital should not be viewed in the narrow context of the business organization. Social capital is about building communities which effectively function with a minimum of conflict.   This is a recipe of an effective organization be it a firm, non-profit organization, government or even a larger society. Segal explains, "The community, whether it is expressed through volunteer activity, in the contexts of recreation, sports, health care, or youth, or in the broader context of institutionalized mandates like universities or hospital boards, is the combination of these absolutely essential expressions of our mutual common interest in shared benefit and experience. Community does what individuals cannot achieve on their own or government can not do as well" (p. 121).

It is easier to create social capital in smaller organizations. Cohesion is most likely when there are fewer interactions and levels of communication. The more homogeneous the group the more likely for shared values and visions. The true test of social entrepreneurship is the creation of social capital for larger and more diverse communities.

The lack of community is cited by Segal as the major cause of social discord. Whether it is conflict among nations or neighbors the lack of trust and other forms of social capital makes reconciliation and progress difficult if not impossible. However delineated, all social organizations face a long agenda of problems crying for solutions. Therein lies the challenge for the social entrepreneur, to be the "bridge builder" creating communities. To do this will require social capital "widening"and well as "deepening". Successful ventures in community building must be translated and transmitted to new situations in the same way technology is transferred.

This process must be accomplished absent the profit motive. Many decades ago, Herzberg's theory stated that employees are motivated not only by monetary rewards. Pay and benefits are only one set of "satisfiers" in Herzberg's eyes. Without pay and benefits comparable to those received by others in similar positions, employees will be dissatisfied, but even the highest pay and greatest array of benefits will bring employees only to a neutral state. Factors such as achievement, recognition, and the work itself take employees past that neutral state into true job satisfaction, motivated to work toward organizational goals.

From the earliest explorations of entrepreneurial psychology summarized by Brockhaus, it has been determined that money was not the ultimate payoff which motivated entrepreneurs. Whether self actualization or the thrill of achievement, social entrepreneurs will work for the common good without the expectation of high salaries, fatter bonuses or additional stock options. Fukuyama found that organizations with a social commitment were more productive with lower turnover, absenteeism and conflict. Civic virtue does appear to have a payoff, but the payoff will not be the principal motivation.

Economists may have something relevant to say about social capital and social entrepreneurship after all. Adam Smith talked about individuals being motivated by "fellow feeling" which was a concern for others which trumped greed and selfishness. For Smith this self sacrificing was the basis for a moral society. In the jargon of today's economists this fellow feeling can be called "interdependent utility" wherein an individual gains pleasure or satisfaction from the activity or consumption of another. (Henderson and Quandt) As parents and grandparents revel in the achievements of their children and sacrifice for them, so individuals can find satisfaction in seeing social ills abated by the creation of social capital. As change agents, social entrepreneurs have to have a calling to rise above narrow self interest.

Perhaps this means revisiting the culture of the Northwest natives of Canada and the United States. Kramer comments regarding their economic and social structure that the upper classes lived a privileged life with the obligation to accumulate wealth. They were then to give it all away in a elaborate ceremony known as potlatch. All benefitted from the success of the few.

12. Social Capital and Public Education

Public elementary and secondary education has been under fire for over a decade. Much of the criticism has focused on poor performance on basic education tests particularly by minority and disadvantaged students. In this discussion there has been little focus on the role K-12 education plays in creating social capital or fostering social entrepreneurship. Public education is a form of social capital, but it also is a creator of those who will become social entrepreneurs. To date there has been virtually no research on how well these functions are being dispatched.

At the very heart of educational reform discussions the concept of social capital should be included. Across the globe curriculum reformers, according to Popkewitz, are concerned less with the specific content of school subjects and more with making the child feel "at home" with a "cosmopolitan identity" that embodies a pragmatic flexibility and "problem-solving" ability (p.5). Pring senses a growing concern for the neglect of personal and social qualities to which teachers and society in general have traditionally attached so much importance: good citizenship, strong values and respect for others. These qualities lead not only to the well being of the individual, but also lead to the growth of social capital.

DeYoung and Theobald believe there is a need to refocus public education. Too often school districts stress what the district needs to get from voters instead of concentrating on how the school can help sustain the social community (Howley, Hadden and Harmon). Elementary and secondary education needs to collaborate with as well as support the community of which it is a part. The two are inexorably tied and dependent on each other. As Fagerlind and Saha conclude, "Education – in the sense of Western-type schooling – is both determined and a determinant of the society of which it is located.... both an agent of change and in turn is changed by society... it acts both as a producer of social mobility and as an agent for the reproduction of the social order" (p.88).

Goldby contends today's school professionals should be expected to foster community relations by working closely with the school's community and by looking upon the school itself as a learning community in which they work to instill a sense of community in their students. This thought is further developed in Lane and Dorfman's definition of collaboration between schools and communities as having two main goals:

1. to strengthen and increase social capital by forming strong social networks; developing active, democratic participation; and fostering a sense of trust and community

2. to increase the ability and capital of the community to utilize stocks of social capital to produce meaningful and sustainable community renewal (p. 10).

Keyes and Gregg state, "...typical discussions of social capital appear to be grounded in the assumption that schools will help people in the community develop social capital and form connections to the school. It would appear that an equal task of collaboration is to develop social capital within the school, by increasing its connections with and trust in the community"(p.6).

How can schools work toward developing desirable social capital? Heretofore, this was expected to be transmitted to children around the family dinner table. Many young people today have never experienced the interweaving and dependency on others that can be found in a close knit family whose relationships are built on trust and communication. Pring comments, "There are certain social skills which we often take for granted, but which have in fact been developed in specific social contexts, in particular, within families who eat together, discuss, question prevailing values, challenge unsubstantiated claims, justify their views when subjected to criticism" (p.86).

Increasingly, K-12 schools are asked to help develop the total person, but the development of social capital is not accomplished within traditional curriculums. Turning to Pring, "The skills and dispositions for so engaging are not easy to acquire, and yet they are either taken for granted or regarded as unimportant in a curriculum which too often pursues a narrow form of academic excellence and a pedagogy which relies on the transmission of unquestioned knowledge" (p.86).

13. Social Capital and Youth Entrepreneurship Education

Research documents a rapid growth of youth entrepreneurship programs in the United States. While these vary in effectiveness and content, all have a central theme of new venture generation and the development of personal entrepreneurial characteristics. In Kourilsky and Carlson's extensive review of entrepreneurship programs focused on youth, there is no mention that social entrepreneurship as a covered topic. The core of entrepreneurship programs they found to be: identification of a market opportunity, generation of a business idea appropriate to the opportunity; the marshaling of resources to pursue the opportunity; the element of risk, and the creation of an operating business based on the idea. Rushing and Kent's review of the penetration of youth entrepreneurship programs in the United States also makes no mention of social entrepreneurship being central to any of the curriculums. Yet there are programs where social entrepreneurship can be found.

Within elementary classrooms, Kourilsky's Mini-Society curriculum has been working toward the development of social entrepreneurship in individuals for more than 20 years (Kourilsky 1996). Taught nationwide in 43 states, the Mini-Society curriculum is an entrepreneurship-based, interdisciplinary instruction system that employs self-organizing, experience-based learning conditions. The Mini-Society instructional system is not a game or a simulation. Fourth, fifth and sixth grade students experience a real world microcosm of society. After the initial stages, the teachers role diminishes to that of a citizen on equal par with the students. As the society develops, students learn to communicate, trust their fellow classmates, and trust their teacher to allow them to make decisions themselves.

During Mini-Society teacher training workshops, teachers are cautioned to let students make their own mistakes and live with the consequences of their decisions as a society. The core values of social capital are essential in the Mini-Society curriculum. Those students who bring high levels of social capital to the classroom can further develop their skills, while other students who may have never had a strong home environment can learn how it feels to be connected to another person and be part of a community based on common values and democratic decision making.

Entrepreneurship education is appealing to high school students as well as elementary school students. A mid 1990's Gallop poll of high school students found 70 percent of them wanting to start a business. Of those wanting to be entrepreneurs, 68 percent felt they would have an obligation to give something back to their communities other than creating jobs. This finding indicates a strong relationship between what is traditionally considered entrepreneurship and "social entrepreneurship" in this age group. Kourilsky and Carlson acknowledge high-school students to be in a "social reformer stage" of their development. This is consistent with the Gallop Poll findings. During secondary education, introduction of social entrepreneurship as part of an entrepreneurship program would seem highly appropriate.

Kourilsky also pioneered another youth entrepreneurship program embracing ideas essential to social entrepreneurship. The EntrePrep program runs for an entire year as an out-of-school experience for rising high-school seniors (Kauffman Center, 1999). Consisting of a summer week of intensive instruction, the participants later engage in an internship with a practicing entrepreneur during the school year. While designed to teach the essentials of business initiation and an appreciation of the importance of entrepreneurial behavior in any situation, the students are also exposed to social entrepreneurship. The students are challenged to consciously consider their personal life goals as well as their future as potential entrepreneurs.

One way in which this is accomplished is by case studies and "elbow rubbing" with practicing entrepreneurs who in addition to being successful business initiators also have been "social capitalists". One outstanding case study is Ewing Marion Kauffman. "Mr. K's" life story is highlighted as a successful entrepreneur who embraced social entrepreneurship by dedicating his life and resources to giving back to his community. His foundation has become a major sponsor of youth entrepreneurship programs, programs for at-risk students and entrepreneurship research. Student's in the EntrePrep Program are taught Kauffman's three guiding principles: treat others as you would like to be treated, those who produce should share the rewards, and give back to the community (Kauffman Center, 2000). These should be emphasized in any youth entrepreneurship curriculum.

14. Conclusions and Future Directions

The authors of this paper have been concerned about the "individualistic" nature of the current academic "discipline" of entrepreneurship. For academics interested in human capital and entrepreneurship educators concerned with innovation, it would be well to remember what Coleman argued. For him social capital has to do with individuals' capacity to relate and associate with each other. This is imperative for economic life and social progress as well. The capacity to form social communities depends on shared values and goals. This allows individuals to subordinate their individuality to a larger group. Shared values lead to trust and trust leads to innovation and economic growth.

Entrepreneurship education programs, at the pre-college or college level, owe it to future entrepreneurs to keep in sight what is most important in innovation today. Above all else, entrepreneurship educators must teach students to value people; their thoughts, abilities and needs. This inclusion must be more than just showing how an individual enterprise can be make more efficient. At the core of the curriculum must be the development of teamwork, interpersonal skills and social consciousness in addition to the techniques and insights needed for venture initiation.

Through people goals are achieved, innovation happens, organizational missions fulfilled and social change transpires. Though the new economy seems different from the old, the values that propelled entrepreneurship in the past will sustain innovative firms through these rapidly changing times. But even more important may be the development of social entrepreneurship healing wounds, reducing tensions and creating a stronger community. Long before the information age, one of history's greatest entrepreneurs, Walt Disney, said, "You can dream, create, design and build the most wonderful place in the world, but it takes people to make the dream a reality". This should be the core for education of social entrepreneurs.

References

Adas, Michael, *Machines as the Measure of Men: Science, Technology, and Ideologies of Western Dominance,* Ithaca: Cornell University Press, (1989).

Blanchard, Ken, *The Heart of a Leader: Insights on the Art of Influence,* Tulsa: Honor Books, (1999).

Brockhaus, Robert H. "The psychology of the entrepreneur" in Calvin Kent, Donald Sexton and Karl Vesper, *Encyclopedia of Entrepreneurship.* Englewood Cliffs NJ: Prentice-Hall, (1982), pp. 39-57.

Brown, John S. and Duguid, Paul, *The Social Life of Information,* Boston: Harvard Business School Press, (2000).

Cohen, Don and Prusak, Laurence, *In Good Company: How Social Capital Makes Organizations Work,* Boston: Harvard Business School Press, (2001).

Coleman, James S. "Social Capital in the Creation of Human Capital," *American Journal of Sociology,* 94 Supplement (1988) S95-S120. and *Foundation of Social Theory,* Cambridge: Harvard University Press, (1995).

Collins, James C., and Collins, Jim, *Good to Great: Why Some Companies Make the Leap and Others Don't,* New York: HarperCollins, (2001).

Coase, R. H., "The Nature of the Firm" reprinted in American Economic Association, *Readings in Price Theory,* Chicago: Irwin, (1952), pp. 331-351.

Curry, Pam, "Growing Microbusinesses: the West Virginia experience" *Mid American Journal of Business.* 16:2, (Fall 2001), pp.7-11.

DeMarco, Tom. *Slack: Getting Past Burnout, Busywork, and the Myth of Total Efficiency,* New York: Random House, (2001).

Disney, Walt, "Just Disney" http;//www. justdisney.com/walt_disney/quotes/ index.html#anchor489570

Duck, Jeanie D., *The Change Monster: The Human Forces that Fuel or Foil Corporate Transformation and Change,* New York: Crown Business Books, (2001).

Fagerlind, I. and Saha, L..J., *Education and National Development: A Comparative Perspective,* Oxford: Pergamon, (1985).

Fukuyama, Francis, *Trust: The Social Virtues and The Creation of Prosperity,* New York: The Free Press, (1995).

Goshal, Sumartra and Bartlett, Christopher, *The Individualized Corporation: A Fundamentally New Approach to Management,* New York: Harper Books, (1999).

Handy, C., *Beyond Certainty: The Changing Worlds of Organisations,* London: Hutchinson, (1995).

Henderson, J. M. and Quandt, R.E., *Microeconomic Theory: A Mathematical Approach,* New York: McGraw-Hill, (1958) pp. 212-214.

Herzberg, F., Mausner, B., and Sayderman, B., *The Motivation to Work,* New York: John Wiley & Sons, (1959).

Howley, C.B., Hadden, P. and Harmon, H., "How These Schools Flourish Differently" in Howley,C., and Harmon, H., *Small High Schools That Flourish,* Charleston, WV: AEL, Inc., (2000).

Kauffman Center, *EntrePrep Curriculum Guide,* Kansas City, MO: Kauffman Center, (1999).

Kauffman Center, *The Philosophies of Mr. K,* Kansas City, MO: Kauffman Center, (2000).

Kelly, Marjorie. *The Divine Right of Capital: Dethroning the Corporate Aristocracy,* San Francisco: Berrett-Koehler, (2001).

Keyes, Marion C. and Gregg, Soleil, "School-Community Connections: A Literature Review" prepared for the Office of Educational Research and Improvement Washington, D.C.,(2001).

Kiley, David, "Crafty basket makers cut downtime, waste", *USA Today,* (May 10, 2001). 3B.

Kotter, John, *Leading Change,* Boston: Harvard Business School Press, (1996).

Kourilsky, Marilyn, *Mini-Society: The Framework,* Kansas City, MO: Kauffman Center, (1996).

Kourilsky, M. L., and Carlson, S. R., "Entrepreneurship Education for Youth: A Curricular Perspective" in Sexton, D.L., and Smilor, R. W., *Entrepreneurship 2000* Chicago: Upstart Publishing, (1997), pp.193-214.

Kramer, Pat. *Totem Poles,* Vancouver B.C. Altitude Publishing, (1995).

Krzyzewski, Mike, *Leading with the Heart: Coach K's Successful Strategies for Basketball, Business and Life*, New York: Warner Books, (2000).

Lane, B. and Dorfman, D., *Strengthening Community Networks: The Basis for Sustainable Community Renewal.* Portland, OR: Northwest Regional Educational Laboratory, (1997).

Locke, John, *The De-Voicing of Society,* New York: Simon and Shuster, (1998).

Longaberger, Dave, *Longaberger; An American Success Story*, New York: HarperCollins,(2001).

Marx, Karl, *Capital*, New York: Random House,(1977), (First published 1883)

Marshall, Edward M., *Building Trust at the Speed of Change: The Power of the Relationship Based Corporation*, New York: AMACOM, (2000).

Narayan, Deepa, *Bonds and Bridges: Social Capital and Poverty,* Washington D.C.: World Bank, (1999).

O'Reilly, C.A. and Pfeffner, Jeffrey, *Hidden Value: How Great Companies Achieve Extraordinary Results with Ordinary People,* Boston: Harvard Business School Press, (2000).

Pope, T. R., Anderson, K.E., and Kramer, J. L., *Federal Taxation 2003*, Upper Saddle River NJ: Prentice-Hall, (2002).

Popkewitz, Thomas S., "Globalization/Regionalization, Knowledge and the Educational Practices" in Popkewitz, Thomas S., *Educational Knowledge,* Albany, State University of New York Press, (2000), pp.3-27.

Pring, Richard, "Citizenship and Schools" in Crick, Bernard, *Citizens: Toward a Citizenship Culture* Oxford Blackwell Publishers, (2001) pp.81-89.

Putnam, Robert D., "The Prosperous Community: Social Capital and Public Life," *American Prospect,* 13 (1993), pp.35-42. and "Bowling Alone," *Journal of Democracy,* 6 (1995) pp.65-78.

Saguaro Seminar, *Social Capital Benchmark Survey; Executive Summary.* Cambridge, MA: John F. Kennedy School of Government, (2001).

Segal, Hugh, *Beyond Greed: A Traditional Conservative Confronts Neoconservative Excess,* Buffalo NY: Stoddart, (1998).

Shutt, Harry, *The Trouble with Capitalism: An Enquiry into the Causes of Global Economic Failure,* New York: St. Martin's, (1998).

Smith, Adam, *The Wealth of Nations*: New York: Penguine Books (1982) (First published 1776)

Smith, T., *Accounting for Growth: Stripping the Camouflage from Company Accounts,* London: Century Business, (1992).

Stewart, Thomas A., *The Wealth of Knowledge: Intellectual Capital and the Twenty -first Century,* New York: Doubleday, (2001)

Woolcox, Michael, "Social Capital and Economic Development: Towards a Theoretical Synthesis and Policy Framework", *Theory and Society*, Vol 27,(1998), pp.151-208.

4. The Multiple Effects of Entrepreneurship on Philanthropy, Society, and Education

William B. Walstad

University of Nebraska-Lincoln

Abstract. Entrepreneurship has unexpected effects on philanthropy, society, and education. Entrepreneurs do not start out to become philanthropists but they often assume that role when a business becomes successful (*direct effect*). Entrepreneurs also enrich their associates and business investors, who also contribute to philanthropic wealth (*indirect effect*). The wealth of entrepreneurs and their associates is the main source of funding for private foundations, which often fund educational initiatives. There is a *feedback effect* from entrepreneurship. More entrepreneurship increases philanthropy, which in turn improves society and education. If this work also improves the business climate for entrepreneurship, there will be more entrepreneurs and wealth. Society and education also benefit from the taxes paid by wealthy entrepreneurs (*tax effect*). Even the consumption of wealthy entrepreneurs partially benefits society through jobs created and taxes paid (*consumption effect*). If an entrepreneur dies before spending all the accumulated wealth, the redistribution process starts over again with the heirs (*inheritance effect*). Finally, there is an *innovative effect*. Entrepreneurial thinking stimulates innovative ways of thinking about philanthropy and how to achieve the best results from the social and educational ventures it supports.

Keywords: entrepreneurs, wealth creation and distribution, philanthropy, foundations, taxation, consumption, inheritance, innovation, and education.

1. Introduction

In 2000, Bill Gates donated $5 billion to the Bill & Melinda Gates Foundation, which was almost half of the $11.1 billion given by the ten largest donors to private charities that year. In 2001, despite the downturn in the technology market, Gates added another $2 billion. This amount was the largest private donation that year and again almost half of the $4.6 billion given by the 10 largest donors to charities. At the end of 2001, the Gates' foundation had an endowment of about $24 billion, making it the nation's largest private foundation. The size of the endowment means that the Gates Foundation must give away about $3.3 million a day, or $1.25 billion per year, to comply with the federal law that it donate 5 percent of its assets on an annual basis.[1] The foundation plans to use these assets to support programs that improve global health care and immunization, fund projects in the public schools, give

---

1.   The data in this paragraph were reported by Kessler (2002) and Houtz (2001).

educational scholarships to minority students, and update the technological resources of libraries.

What is remarkable is that when Bill Gates started Microsoft with Paul Allen in 1975, he never expected to become the world's biggest philanthropist. At that time his focus was on creating BASIC software for different types of computers such as Altair, Apple, Commodore, and Radio Shack. By 1979, the year the firm moved to Seattle, the company consisted of only 12 employees. The big break came in 1981 when Microsoft was invited to produce the MS-DOS system to run IBM PCs. Within seven years, the firm became the largest producer of computer software and had expanded its workforce to 20,000.[2] In 2001, although Microsoft ranked 72nd on the *Fortune* list of the largest 500 U.S. corporations, with revenues of $25.2 billion, it ranked second in its market capitalization at about $331.5 billion.[3] Bill Gates' stake in Microsoft stock gave him a net worth of $52.8 billion in 2001, making him the richest person in the world.[4]

The transition from struggling entrepreneur to super wealthy philanthropist is not a story that is unique to Bill Gates. The same story can be found in the biographical history of one of the foremost entrepreneurs of the late nineteenth century – Andrew Carnegie.[5] Carnegie was born in 1835 as the son of a poor Scottish weaver, who emigrated with his family to the United States in 1847. His hard work, self-education, and entrepreneurial insights led him into the bridge-making business when iron was the main type of material used for construction. He then incorporated the use of steel as the basic construction material with the 1864 introduction of the Bessemer process for transforming iron into steel. From that experience he figured out how to build steel plants that improved the production efficiency in that new industry and made his fortune. In 1901 he sold his company for $480 million to U.S. Steel, a company controlled by the wealth financier, J.P. Morgan.

After retiring in his sixties, Carnegie spent the remaining 18 years of his life giving his fortune away to support libraries and other projects.[6] The amount of wealth that Carnegie amassed over his lifetime was estimated to be about $475 million (about $4.9 billion in 2002 dollars).[7] He gave away more than $350 million and established an endowment of $125 million to create the nation's first philanthropic foundation, which is still in existence and bears his name. In his philanthropic work, Carnegie was following his principles for the

---

2.   For the source of this early history, see Hallett and Hallett (1997).
3.   See *Fortune* (2002) for data on the largest corporations.
4.   Kroll and Goldman (2002), p. 120.
5.   The information on Carnegie that follows is largely obtained from Klepper and Gunther (1996), pp. 29-33, and Tedlow (2001), pp. 19-71.
6.   The improvement of libraries was also the first philanthropic interest of Bill Gates.
7.   The $475 million estimate is from Klepper and Gunther (1996, pp. 29-33) valued at Carnege's death in 1919. The 2002 estimate adjusts the $475 million for inflation based on the average Consumer Price Index and using the CPI calculator at http://www.bls.gov.

social responsibility of the rich that he had set forth in his essay on "The Gospel of Wealth."[8] In this essay, he exhorted the wealthy to give away most of their fortune within their lifetime rather than wait until death to make the redistribution and also be actively involved in the philanthropic work: "surplus wealth should be considered as a sacred trust to be administered by those into whose hands it falls, during their lives, for the good of the community."[9]

The other classic example of the entrepreneur turned philanthropist of the late nineteenth century was John D. Rockefeller. In 1863, he started on the path to creating an empire in the oil refining business. Through a combination of management discipline, cost efficiency, and various business schemes, he expanded the reach of Standard Oil so that by 1880 it controlled 95 percent of the oil refining in the United States. Rockefeller's wealth accumulated with the rising monopoly power of Standard Oil and totaled about $1.4 billion over his life (about $17.5 billion in 2002 dollars). What is often forgotten is that Rockefeller basically retired from running Standard Oil in 1887, and devoted his full-time attention to philanthropic activities until his death in 1937. He also tithed ten percent of his income to the church throughout his life and donated half a billion dollars to various projects and causes. He left a legacy of almost half a billion dollars to his son, who also spent most of his life giving away money, as have the six offspring of John D., Jr.[10] The Rockefeller name, first synonymous with great wealth, is now equally recognized for its lasting and continuing contribution to philanthropy.

There are, of course, many other examples of generous entrepreneurs who made fortunes and gave large portions of them away, either during their lifetimes or at their deaths. George Soros, a Hungarian immigrant, made his estimated $6.9 billion fortune forming a hedge fund and taking risks as a hedge fund trader. He has donated over $2 billion to the development of open societies in Russia and central and eastern European nations.[11] Gordon Moore, the founder of Intel, has an estimated net worth of $6.1 billion as of March 2002. He and his wife reportedly donated or pledged a similar amount as Soros to education and scientific research projects. There are also many entrepreneurs with less substantial fortunes, who nonetheless give away a significant percentage of the wealth that they created as entrepreneurs.

---

8. For the essay and details about it, see the Carnegie (1889/1992) chapter in an edited book on philanthropy and wealth by Burlingame (1992).
9. The quote is from Riley (1992), p. 68.
10. The data cited in this paragraph are from Klepper and Gunther, p. 7.
11. The data on net worth is from Kroll and Goldman (2002). The data on lifetime giving is reported in Albo (1999).

2. Direct and Indirect Effects

The above examples, and others too numerous to describe, illustrate how the amount of philanthropy in the United States is directly influenced by entrepreneurship and the wealth it creates. The capitalist system gives people the profit incentive to form businesses. If the start-up business is ultimately successful, which is by no means guaranteed in this profit and loss system, then the entrepreneur can accumulate wealth, often far beyond the initial expectations or forecasts at the beginning of the business. What is unexpected is that entrepreneurs do not go into business to start foundations or have social impact. They go into business to be their own boss, to put their skills and abilities to best use, to create a new product from a perceived opportunity, or for some other reason.[12] They do not start a business primarily because they can give their wealth to charities or to start a foundation that will redistribute their wealth for them. That philanthropic role, if the entrepreneur accepts it, comes as a consequence of business success, and gets thrust upon an entrepreneur as one possible answer to what to do with their abundance of riches.

What is forgotten in the media attention given to the entrepreneurial stars are the indirect effects of entrepreneurship on philanthropy. The amount of the wealth created by entrepreneurs such as Bill Gates, Warren Buffett, Larry Ellison, Sam Walton, Michael Dell, and Pierre Omidyar is significantly larger than their individual net worth.[13] There are business associates who helped the business grow during its start-up period or who invested in the business during its early development, and they also became rich along with the founder. For every entrepreneur who started a successful business and amassed a fortune, there are hundreds of other business associates and investors who become sufficiently wealthy from the work of the entrepreneur that they too have the choice of making significant philanthropic contributions. Entrepreneurship has a wealth-creating direct effect on the business founder and a wealth-creating indirect effect on major associates and investors enriched by the business. This indirect effect expands the pool of wealth far beyond that amassed by the business founder alone. These funds become the source for even more philanthropic activities in society.[14]

The strong connection between entrepreneurship and philanthropy is often unrecognized. Historians and other biographical writers primarily focus on the business practices and methods of the entrepreneur as the firm grows, while the philanthropic contribution of the entrepreneur is a secondary story because it

---

12. For a list of such reasons, see Walstad and Kourilsky (1999), pp. 21, 28. For biographical sketches of the motivations for successful entrepreneurs, see Mariotti and Caslin (2000).
13. Although Buffett is often thought of only as an investor, his investment and management strategies in the development of Berkshire Hathaway are innovative and entrepreneurial (Miles, 2001).

comes after the business has prospered.[15] What is often neglected in these histories and biographies is that successful entrepreneurship creates the unexpected opportunity for the entrepreneur to do something else with a life in addition to working in the business. It is this philanthropic opportunity that allows an entrepreneur to find an innovative way to improve society and build a reputation that is unrelated to the initial business success and might have a legacy that extends longer than the business.[16] Some entrepreneurs, such as Carnegie, accepted this philanthropic opportunity during their lifetimes; others, such as Sam Walton, preferred to focus on expanding their profit-making business and left the philanthropic opportunity to a foundation or family heirs after their deaths.

3. Feedback Effect

If philanthropy, and all it does to improve society is to be encouraged, then there needs to be more in entrepreneurship because it will create more philanthropy. The philanthropic work in turn should improve the society in which people live and work. This improvement in the society should enhance the educational system and the business climate and support for entrepreneurship. And if more entrepreneurship can be stimulated as society advances, there is a feedback effect from entrepreneurship that reinforces the process. Figure 1 below shows the connections:

---

14. Carnegie recognized the importance of surrounding himself with good associates, and did so with Charles M. Schwab and Henry Frick. He once remarked that his epitaph should read: "Here lies a man who was able to surround himself with men far cleverer than himself" (Klepper and Gunther, 1996, p. 31). It should not be surprising that along with Bill Gates on the *Forbes* list are Paul Allen and Steve Ballmer. Entrepreneurship creates wealth for the founders and their associates.
15. See commentary about historians by Johnson (1999). See commentary about the media by Saal (1997). For an example of biographies with minimal attention to the philanthropy of successful entrepreneurs, see Tedlow (2001).
16. An entrepreneur may decide to become a philanthropist for many reasons, such as an altruistic desire to give something back to people, perhaps to make amends for past business practices and improve public image, or because of tax incentives. The various motivations for the decision to become a philanthropist will vary by individual and is beyond the scope of this discussion, although it has been a topic of interest to historians, psychologists, and economists. For an economic analysis of the effects of tax changes on the philanthropy of the rich, see Slemrod (2000).

Figure 1: Feedback Connections

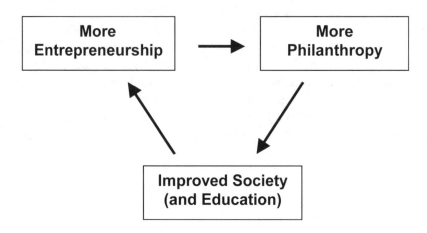

The major elements of this feedback loop can be seen in the U.S. economic experience since the industrialization of the mid-to-late 1880s. The United States has a long history of encouraging entrepreneurship, supporting economic freedom, and accepting technological change.[17] Given this business climate, entrepreneurship was able to flourish and great wealth was created. It should not be surprising that as the nation has become wealthier, the number of private charitable foundations grew from the one first started by Andrew Carnegie with $125 million in 1919 to over 50,000 foundations with an asset base of $449 billion in 1999.[18] Some of these foundations are large in asset size and others are small, but regardless of the size many private foundations in the United States are based on the donated wealth of entrepreneurs or their families. The not-for-profit sector thrives in the United States because entrepreneurs have been given an opportunity to thrive and prosper in this nation.[19] This entrepreneurship-to-philanthropy relationship is evident in the

---

17. For data on the positive business climate for entrepreneurship in the United States in comparison to other nations, see Reynolds, et al. (2001).
18. These 1999 data are the latest available from the Foundation Center. The assets, however, are not equally distributed across the foundations. Of the 50,000 foundations, there are only 206 with assets of more than $250 million. These foundations account for 53 percent of all foundation assets.
19. The importance of entrepreneurs to wealth creation should not be understated. It has been estimated that entrepreneurs account for 68 percent of the net worth held by the top 1 percent of households in the distribution of wealth in the United States (Hubbard, 2000, p. 456). For discussion of the taxes and its effects on the philanthropy of the wealthy, see Auten, Clotfelter, and Schmalbeck (2000).

names and industries associated with the most of the top 50 largest foundations in the United States, as shown in Table 1.

Table 1: Top 50 U.S. Foundations by Asset Size

Rank	Name/(state)	Assets (in billion $)	Funding Source (Industry)
1. Bill & Melinda Gates Foundation (WA)		$ 21.1	software
2. Lilly Endowment Inc. (IN)		15.6	pharmaceuticals
3. The Ford Foundation (NY) (1)		14.7	autos
4. J. Paul Getty Trust (CA) (2)		10.9	oil
5. The David and Lucile Packard Foundation (CA)		9.8	computers
6. The Robert Wood Johnson Foundation (NJ)		8.8	medical supplies
7. W. K. Kellogg Foundation (MI) (3)		5.7	cereal
8. The Andrew W. Mellon Foundation (NY)		4.9	banking
9. The Pew Charitable Trusts (PA)		4.8	oil
10. The Starr Foundation (NY) (4)		4.5	insurance
11. John D. and Catherine T. MacArthur Foundation (IL)		4.5	insurance
12. The William and Flora Hewlett Foundation (CA)		3.9	computers
13. The Rockefeller Foundation (NY)		3.6	oil
14. The California Endowment (CA) (5)		3.5	———
15. Robert W. Woodruff Foundation, Inc. (GA)		3.1	soft drink
16. The Annie E. Casey Foundation (MD)		3.0	parcel delivery
17. The Annenberg Foundation (PA) (6)		2.9	media
18. Charles Stewart Mott Foundation (MI)		2.9	autos
19. The Duke Endowment (NC)		2.9	tobacco
20. Casey Family Programs (WA)		2.8	parcel delivery
21. The Kresge Foundation (MI)		2.8	retail
22. John S. and James L. Knight Foundation (FL)		2.2	newspapers
23. The Freeman Foundation (NY)		2.1	———
24. The Harry and Jeanette Weinberg Foundation, Inc. (MD) (5)		2.1	———
25. Ewing Marion Kauffman Foundation (MO) (6)		2.0	pharmaceuticals
26. The McKnight Foundation (MN)		2.0	manufacturing
27. The New York Community Trust (NY)		1.9	———
28. Carnegie Corporation of New York (NY) (1)		1.9	steel
29. Richard King Mellon Foundation (PA)		1.9	banking
30. Robert R. McCormick Tribune Foundation (IL)		1.9	newspapers
31. Wallace-Readers Digest Funds (NY)		1.6	publishing
32. The Cleveland Foundation (OH)		1.6	———
33. Doris Duke Charitable Foundation (NY)		1.6	tobacco
34. W. M. Keck Foundation (CA)		1.5	oil
35. The James Irvine Foundation (CA)		1.5	ranch land
36. Houston Endowment Inc. (TX)		1.5	———
37. Alfred P. Sloan Foundation (NY)		1.4	autos
38. The Brown Foundation, Inc. (TX) (6)		1.3	construction
39. The Packard Humanities Institute (CA)		1.3	computer hardware
40. The Chicago Community Trust and Affiliates (IL) (1)		1.3	———
41. Donald W. Reynolds Foundation (NV)		1.3	media
42. The William Penn Foundation (PA)		1.2	———
43. Marin Community Foundation (CA) (6)		1.2	———
44. Freedom Forum, Inc. (VA) (4)		1.1	———
45. The Henry Luce Foundation, Inc. (NY)		1.1	publishing
46. The Anschutz Foundation (CO) (7)		1.1	gas, oil
47. The California Wellness Foundation (CA)		1.0	———
48. Howard Heinz Endowment (PA)		1.0	food products
49. The Joyce Foundation (IL)		1.0	lumber
50. Walton Family Foundation, Inc. (AR)		1.0	retailing

Source: Asset data are reported at: http://www.foundationcenter.org/research/trends_analysis/top100assets.html. The data are for the fiscal year ending 12/31/00, unless indicated by the numbers following the foundation name: (1) [09/30/00]; (2) [06/30/00]; (3) [08/31/01]; (4) [12/31/99]; (5) [02/28/01]; (6) [06/30/01]; (7) [11/30/00]. The initial funding for the foundation by industry is based on author research.

3.1. Education and Assets

The education sector is a major beneficiary of the grant funding from foundations. Almost a quarter (24.4 percent) of the $11.6 billion in 1999 grants from foundations went to education. The education category was larger by a third to a half over other major grant categories such as health (17.2 percent), human services (16.2 percent) or arts and culture (13.4 percent).[20] Of the $2.8 billion given by foundations to education that year, well over half (62 percent) went to higher education, a quarter (25 percent) was spent on projects in elementary and secondary schools, and the remainder (13 percent) went to libraries or an assortment of educational services.[21]

Entrepreneurship indirectly influences education because it serves as the initial source of assets for many foundations, which in turn devote a major portion of their assets to grant-making at all levels of education.[22] This wealth also funds new initiatives in education. In higher education, for example, the Gates Foundation pledged $1 billion over 20 years for financial aid for minority students so that they can attend colleges and universities. At the pre-college level, Ted Forstmann and John Walton gave $100 million to establish a foundation to obtain matching funding for scholarships for low-income students to attend private schools. Solving problems in education will always be an appealing target for wealthy entrepreneurs.

There is a compound interest from entrepreneurship for education or any other area of philanthropic interest of a foundation started by an entrepreneur. By law, foundations must give five percent of their assets in grants each year. If, however, a foundation can earn more than five percent on the assets of the foundation, then it can slowly increase the asset base and this will allow the foundation to give more to education or other philanthropic concerns. Over time, prudent investing of the foundation assets has the potential to permit donations to projects in excess of the asset base left by the entrepreneurs or heirs. For illustration purposes, let's say a $1 billion foundation gives away $50 million a year (5 percent). Assume that the foundation is also able to earn $100 million on its assets (10 percent or around the long-term return on stock

---

20. The remaining categories were environment and animals (6.3 percent), international affairs (3 percent), science and technology (3.6 percent), social sciences (2.3 percent), religion (2.3 percent) and other (0.1 percent). The data are from the Foundation Center (1999).

21. The higher education estimate is based on combining grants for higher education (47 percent) and grants for graduate and professional education (15 percent). Foundation Center (2001).

22. It is not only foundations that give significantly to education. Wealthy individuals give a disproportionate share of their gifts to education. Auten, Clotfelter, and Schmalbeck (2000) obtained data on 90 individuals who gave $5 million or more in 1996. Higher education (non-medical portion) received 56 percent of the gifts. Successful entrepreneurs have a history of giving to education even if they never completed high school or college. See Tedlow (2001), pp. 431-433, for examples from Andrew Carnegie, George Eastman, Thomas Watson, and Bill Gates.

equities). At the end of the year the asset base of the foundation has increased from $1 billion to $1.05 billion, which means that next year the foundation can make $52.5 million in grants. If a similar process occurs over time, the foundation assets will significantly increase the philanthropic giving.

3.2. A Weak Link?

The most difficult connection to understand in the circular flow is not the one from entrepreneurship and philanthropy, or the obvious connection between philanthropy and an improved society, but the connection from an improved society to having more entrepreneurship. Here the link can be broken unless the improvements to society and education lead to changes in the business climate so it supports and encourages more entrepreneurship. Such immediate actions as improving the access to start-up capital for all entrepreneurs, and especially for women and minorities, will increase the number of entrepreneurs in all sectors and regions of the economy. It is also important to find ways to reduce the cost of government regulations and red tape so that they do not place an undue burden on smaller start-up businesses relative to larger corporations. Tax laws can be simplified to reduce the compliance cost, and tax rates can be cut to encourage more business investment. These policies are just a few of the ones proposed to enhance the business climate to help small businesses and stimulate more entrepreneurship.[23]

Our society also needs to give significantly more attention to entrepreneurship education at all ages. Too few youth and young adults receive an education that develops their entrepreneurial thinking and venturing capabilities. There is abundant evidence of strong interest in entrepreneurship among youth and young adults, but the current curriculum in both schools and colleges does not begin to prepare them with the basic knowledge and skills they need. This entrepreneurship education is important for both future entrepreneurs and others who do not become entrepreneurs. It will certainly expand the number of people who might start a business because they will have the initial preparation and encouragement they need to take the risk of becoming an entrepreneur. For other students, an education in entrepreneurship helps them learn to think in entrepreneurial terms, which can help them in whatever activities or careers they select during their lives. Perhaps most important, this type of education makes people generally more understanding and supportive of those who make a new venture successful, regardless of whether the enterprise is in the profit or non-profit sector.[24]

---

23. See proposals from the National Federation of Independent Business (NFIB) which is available at: http://www.nfib.com.

4. Tax Effect: Education Benefit

Until this point, the working assumption was that the wealth the entrepreneur creates from a successful business was either used to establish a foundation or donated to a charitable cause of interest to the entrepreneur. This accounting, however, does not reveal the full story of what happens to wealth created from a successful business and how it can affect society and education. There is a tax effect from entrepreneurship that takes some of the wealth. The entrepreneur will be taxed at the local, state, and federal levels during a lifetime.[25] The earnings of the entrepreneur's corporation will also be taxed, generally at the state or federal level. If the entrepreneur dies without giving away all the wealth, then what remains will be taxed as part of the entrepreneur's estate. How much tax is paid by an entrepreneur while living and at death, or what amount of tax will be paid by the entrepreneur's corporation, will depend on complex tax laws and individual or business circumstances.

What then happens to the portion of the entrepreneur's wealth that is taxed is another complex story. The funds that flow into the coffers of the federal, state, or local government will be spent on government programs. At the state and local level, a good portion of the taxed income or wealth will wind up in the education sector. About 22 percent of the general expenditures of states are for education. Over 43 percent of the general expenditures for local government are for education. Taxes paid at the federal level will go primarily for pensions and income security, health, and national defense, but about 15 percent of the revenue transferred from the federal to state governments is for education.[26] To the extent that entrepreneurial income or wealth goes to pay taxes, education directly benefits from this transfer from private to public uses.

5. Consumption Effect: Taxes and Jobs

The consumption expenditures of successful entrepreneurs have a positive influence on society in several indirect ways. First, most consumption expenditures will be taxed either through sales taxes or property taxes. These taxes will become another source of revenue for government programs, especially at the state and local levels, a good portion of which goes for

---

24. For further discussion and data on points made in this paragraph about how entrepreneurship education can contribute to entrepreneurship, see Walstad and Kourilsky (1999) and Kourilsky and Walstad (2000).
25. Another indirect effect from entrepreneurship would be the taxes paid by the entrepreneurs' employees, but this issue will not be considered here because the purpose is to track what happens to the entrepreneurs' wealth.
26. U.S. Census Bureau (2001, Table 224, p. 267 and Table 225, p. 268).

education funding.[27] Second, there are jobs created and supported by the consumption expenditures of the wealthy entrepreneurs. Although there can be a normative debate about whether these are the jobs that should be created in the economy, there is no need to argue about whether jobs are generated from this personal spending by wealthy entrepreneurs. The entrepreneur will spend some portion of disposable income (or accumulated wealth) for personal consumption on such items as food, clothing, housing, transportation, and an array of personal services. There is the mistaken belief that the wealthy spend all of their incomes on a high life style when surveys of the wealthy and other research indicate that it is often not the case. The problem is that the income and consumption relationship needs to be viewed in relative rather than in the absolute or dollar terms that gets the media attention. In economics, it has long been known that the average propensity to consume an income declines as incomes increase. This relationship means that high-income individuals (often the wealthy entrepreneurs) will save, on average, a higher proportion of their incomes compared with lower-income individuals. The high-income individuals are then able to use their savings to increase their net worth by investing in income-producing assets, a tendency that is especially present among struggling entrepreneurs seeking to "grow" their businesses.

6. Inheritance Effect: Accounting and Redistribution

Another avenue needs to be explored for a full accounting of what happens to the wealth created by the entrepreneurs. Some entrepreneurs may decide not to donate much of their wealth to charity or establish a private foundation to receive their funds either while they are living or at their death. They may instead decide to pass the bulk of their wealth to their family in the form of trust or other bequeathing arrangements. It may appear that in this case there are no societal effects from this portion of the wealth created by the entrepreneur. The conclusion, however, is not a valid one. The shifting of the entrepreneur's assets to other people only shifts the timing of when the wealth will be redistributed and when it will have its impact on society.[28]

There are many cases of entrepreneurs who gave most of their wealth to their family instead of directly to society, and yet that wealth is not lost to

---

27. Stanley and Danko (1996, pp. 27-69) describe the frugality of the wealthy based on their surveys and interviews with the wealthy, many of whom were entrepreneurs.
28. Inheritances can have negative effects. Andrew Carnegie made the conjuncture that "parents who leave their children enormous wealth generally deaden their children's talents and energies and tempt them to lead less productive lives." Holtz-Eakin, Joulfaian, and Rosen (1993) found support for this conjecture. Larger inheritance led people to leave the labor force, and among those who stay, their incomes grow slower than others without inheritances, perhaps because they worked few hours or reduced their work effort.

society. It just remains unspent and is not yet redistributed. Consider the case of Sam Walton. He amassed a fortune estimated to be $22 billion in 1991, the year before he died, but had it divided into shares for his wife and four children. By 2002, the collective wealth of the five Walton heirs had grown to just over $100 billion, or about $20 billon each.[29]   The family members will be redistributing some of that wealth through the Walton Family Foundation, which made a recent gift of $500 million to the University of Arkansas. The responsibility of redistributing the wealth and making sure that it has a meaningful impact on education or society was shifted from the original entrepreneur to the entrepreneur's family. The amount that the Waltons have to redistribute is so enormous that it will likely be shifted to the third or fourth generation of the Walton family, as was the case with the Rockefeller wealth in spite of the substantial philanthropic giving by John D. Rockefeller and John D. Rockefeller, Jr.

The major avenues for the redistribution of wealth are summarized in Figure 2. Perhaps the easiest way to think about the matter is to start with the net worth of the entrepreneur and ask what happens to the net worth of that individual over time. Some of that net worth is transferred to philanthropy through charitable gifts or through philanthropic foundations and is used to benefit society. Some net worth (or the income that generates it) is taxed. Those funds also benefit society by paying for public goods and services. Consumption expenditures either from income or accumulated wealth have some minor benefit for society because they provide more tax revenues and create jobs. Finally, a portion of the net worth that is amassed over time will be left to family members or other beneficiaries.   For this group, the redistribution cycle starts over again because they face the same decisions as the initial entrepreneurs about wealth allocation or additions to net worth. All four avenues of wealth redistribution have an impact on the society.

Figure 2: Redistributing the Wealth of Successful Entrepreneurs

Starting Point	Allocation	Impact
	→ Philanthropy	→ Society through gifts and foundations
Net Worth of Entrepreneur	→ Taxes	→ Society through funding of public goods and services
	→ Consumption	→ Personal, but some social through taxes paid or jobs created
	→ Family (heirs)	→ Return to starting point (Net Worth)

---

29. Kroll and Goldman (2002), p. 20.

7. Innovation Effect

One of the powerful outcomes from entrepreneurship is that it serves as the source of innovation in ways of conducting business that had not been tried before or been very effective in the past. Such an innovation effect can be seen in the approach to wealth redistribution via philanthropy. The most commonly used approach and the one with the longest history is for the donor to give a gift or grant directly to a worthy group or organization, be it a homeless shelter or a university. During the early part of the past century, with the growth of great entrepreneurial fortunes, the establishment of a philanthropic foundation became the popular means for redistributing great wealth. The entrepreneur's role in the leadership and management of these foundations could be active or passive depending on the founder's preferences and the timing of the major donations (during the life of the entrepreneur or after). The foundation would then solicit grant proposals that met the foundation's objectives and fund the project evaluated to be most worthy, be it funding for the local symphony or support for an after-school youth program. The grantee would then use the funding for the designated purpose, but there would not be active intervention by the foundation in management of the project. This approach to giving is considered to be the "traditional" type of philanthropy.

In the past decade, experiences with entrepreneurship in the high-tech sector led some newly minted millionaires and billionaires to rethink how they wanted to give away their wealth. What they conceived was a new and more entrepreneurial method for charitable giving called venture philanthropy. This approach involves applying the investing and management practices that venture capitalists use for start-up businesses to the allocation and management of charitable funding. The venture philanthropist would invest in those projects with clearly outlined business plans that would have the greatest social return. The venture philanthropists would be investing in "social" entrepreneurs, who would be responsible for delivering measurable results based on performance objectives or they would lose their funding. For their part, the venture philanthropists would help make the projects successful because they would contribute their skills and management expertise along with their funds. This transfer of expertise in funding and management would make the nonprofit sector more entrepreneurial and insure that the projects created social value.

Pierre Omidyar, the 34-year-old founder of E-bay, provides a good example of this new approach to philanthropy. He and his wife Pam were estimated to have a net worth of $4.6 billion as of March 2002. They plan to give away all but one percent of their wealth by 2020, but they want to make sure that it makes a difference to society. Hardy (2000) describes their mission as radical philanthropy: "Just as Webheads demolished old business models, Pierre and Pam Omidyar strive to demolish philanthropic models in favor of new ones that deliver on the very elusive goal of all grant givers, accountability" (p. 115). They established the Omidyar Foundation and it funds groups and organizations for longer periods than is the case for traditional charities. The conditions they require the philanthropic organizations to meet to receive funding are similar to what a venture capitalist would demand of a start-up firm. There must be a solid business plan, an important problem (opportunity) to be addressed, and the organization must meet accountability targets showing it having an impact by creating value for the community.[30]

Some of the enthusiasm for this new approach waned with the collapse of the high-tech sector because there is less available funding for these philanthropic initiatives. There are other significant reasons for the decline in enthusiasm for this new approach. Some of the wealthy entrepreneurs or foundation leaders who adopted this approach now realize that they did not have the sufficient foundation staff or time to provide the strategic management needed by the nonprofits. The nonprofits were also not always able to make the best use of the management expertise that was provided.

Of particular importance is that there is more realism about what can be accomplished through venture or even traditional philanthropy. Solving social problems and creating social value, whether in health care or education, is significantly more complicated and complex than solving business problems and creating market value. In this situation it is easy to oversell the benefits of the new philanthropic work and not be shown dramatic results. Perhaps indicative of this change in thinking about venture philanthropy was an industry report that was overly optimistic for its promise in 2000, the height of the tech bubble, but was equivocal in 2001: "It remains too early to demonstrate that venture philanthropy results in more effective outcomes or more powerful social change in ways that distinguish it from traditional philanthropy."[31]

The experiments in applying concepts and methods from entrepreneurship to make philanthropy more effective are far from over. Venture philanthropy and social entrepreneurship offer a new approach to charitable giving that in certain situations and contexts may prove to be more effective than other philanthropic approaches for addressing social or educational problems. This approach has sparked a re-thinking among wealthy entrepreneurs and

---

30. This description of the Omidyars' approach to philanthropy is based on the story by Hardy (2000). The net worth estimated comes from Kroll and Goldman (2002). Another story of venture philanthropy can be found in Dowie (1999) who describes the activities of George Roberts of the KKR leveraged-buyout firm. Streisand (2001) provides another story of venture philanthropy.
31. The quote is from a commentary by Colvin (2001) in *Fortune* that is critical of the hype surrounding venture philanthropy. He also observes that "giving money effectively can be harder than making it" (p. 50).

traditional philanthropies of the best way to make the nonprofit sector more accountable and create more social value from philanthropy.

The entrepreneurial experiences in the U.S. economy over the past two decades produced a new model for thinking about how to make more efficient social use of the scarce resources available from philanthropy. Education will be a prime beneficiary of this innovative effect because of major public concern with improving the nation's schools, colleges, and universities. In entrepreneurship it only takes one or two successful models to radically alter an entire industry or ways of thinking about past practices. That possibility is present in education and with other social issues as experiments in philanthropy continue into the next decade.

8. Conclusion

Entrepreneurship has the power to transform society to a much greater extent than is commonly thought. Most people see that transformation only in terms of the new business innovations or products that come to market and alter what businesses produce and what consumers buy. What is often not recognized are the multiple effects of entrepreneurship on philanthropy, and in turn on society and education.

Without philanthropy, the major source of funding for societal or educational improvement would come exclusively from government funding. Philanthropy allows for a much wider range of ideas, choices, and programs to improve society compared with what is possible through government legislation and public budgeting. Philanthropy also achieves its objectives with more speed, flexibility, and targeting than is often possible through public decision-making or the control of government officials. The diversity in philanthropy enriches and expands opportunities to improve social life in much the same way as diversity in markets enriches and expands economic life.[32]

Each new generation of wealthy entrepreneurs will bring their innovative approaches to how best to redistribute their wealth so that it best benefits society. Andrew Carnegie considered those decisions and came up with innovative practices when he started to give away his wealth at the end of the nineteenth century. Some of the new wealthy entrepreneurs are re-thinking how to make effective use of their wealth to address the social and educational issues of the twenty-first century. The answers may be different over generations of entrepreneurs, but the powerful innovative effect of

---

32. For a discussion of the importance of diversity to economic life and markets, see Rosen (2002).

entrepreneurship on philanthropy, and the experiments it unleashes in society and education, will be ever-present and reinforcing.

Although entrepreneurship is often referred to as the "engine" of economic growth, it should also be considered the "engine" of philanthropy. An increase in the number of successful entrepreneurs means that there will be an increase in the available funding for philanthropic ventures. In this way, the profit-making activity of entrepreneurs that generates private wealth has direct and indirect benefits to society. Education, as a major focus of social concern, stands to gain from the philanthropic largess of entrepreneurs and the transfer of wealth that is expected to increase over the next few decades.

References

Albo, A. (1999, April). "The benefactor 1002." *Worth*, 8(4) pp. 110-122.

Auten, G.E., Clotfelter, C.T., & Schmalbeck, R.L. (2000). "Taxes and philanthropy among the wealthy". In J.B. Slemrod. (Ed.), *Does Atlas shrug? The economic consequences of taxing the rich* (pp. 392-424). New York: Russell Sage Foundation.

Burlingame, D.F. (Ed.). (1992). *The responsibilities of wealth.* Bloomington, IN: Indiana University Press.

Carnegie, A. (1992). "The gospel of wealth." In D.F. Burlingame (Ed.), *The responsibilities of wealth*, pp. 1-31. Bloomington, IN: Indiana University Press. (Original work published 1889.)

Colvin, G. (2001, December 24). "The gift of arrogance." *Fortune, 144*(13), p. 50.

Dowie, M. (1999, February). "Venture philanthropy." *Worth*, 8(2), pp. 68-71.

Fortune. (2002, April 15). The five hundred largest U.S. corporations, p. F-3.

Foundation Center. (1999). *Foundation giving trends.* New York: Foundation Center.

Foundation Center. (2001). *Foundation giving trends* [On-line]. Available: http://fdncenter.org/research/trends_analysis/pdf/02fgthl.pdf.

Hallett, A., & Hallett, D. (1997). *Encyclopedia of entrepreneurs.* New York: John Wiley and Sons.

Hardy, Q. (2000, May 5). "The radical philanthropist." *Forbes, 165*(10), pp. 114-122.

Holtz-Eakin, D., Joulfaian, D., & Rosen, H.S. (1993, May). "The Carnegie conjecture: Some empirical evidence". *Quarterly Journal of Economics, 108*(2) pp. 413-436.

Houtz, J. (2001, November 11). "Gates Foundation wields newfound clout". *The San Diego Union-Tribune*, p. E3.

Hubbard, G. (2000). "Commentary on chapter 13." In J.B. Slemrod (Ed.), *Does Atlas shrug? The economic consequences of taxing the rich* (pp. 456-461). New York: Russell Sage Foundation.

Johnson, P. (1999). "The prospering fathers." *Commentary, 108*(1) (July/August), pp. 66-68.

Kessler, M. (2002, January 3). "Tech stock drops hits charities' bottom line." *USA Today*, p. 3B).

Klepper, M., & Gunther, R. (1996). *The wealthy 100: From Benjamin Franklin to Bill Gates— A ranking of the richest Americans, past and present.* Secaucus, NJ: Carol Publishing Group.

Kourilsky, M.L., & Walstad, W.B. (2000). *The "E" generation: Prepared for the entrepreneurial economy?* Dubuque, IA: Kendall/Hunt Publishing.

Kroll, L., & Goldman, L. (2002, March 18). "The global billionaires". *Forbes*, pp. 119-152.

Mariotti, S., & Caslin, M. (2000). *The very very rich: How they got that way, and how you can too.* Franklin Lakes, NJ: The Career Press.

Miles, R.P. (2001). *The Warren Buffett CEO: Secrets of the Berkshire Hathaway managers.* New York: John Wiley.

Reynolds, P.D, Camp, M.S., Bygrave, W.D., Autio, E., & Hay, M. (2001). *Global entrepreneurship monitor: 2001 summary report.* London and Boston: London Business School and Babson College.

Riley, J. (1992). "Philanthropy under capitalism." In Burlingame, D.F. (Ed.), *The responsibilities of wealth* (pp. 66-93). Bloomington, IN: Indiana University Press.

Rosen, S. (2002). "Markets and diversity." *American Economic Review, 92*(1) (March), pp. 1-15.

Saal, H. (1997, September 22). "New list for the wealthy." *Newsweek, 130*(12), p. 14.

Slemrod, J.B. (Ed.). (2000). *Does Atlas shrug? The economic consequences of taxing the rich.* New York: Russell Sage Foundation.

Stanley, T.J., & Danko, W.D. (1996). *The millionaire next door: The surprising secrets of America's wealthy.* Atlanta, Georgia: Longstreet Press.

Streisand, B. (2001, June 11). "The new philanthropy." *U.S. News & World Report, 130*(23), pp. 40-43.

Tedlow, R.S. (2001). *Giants of enterprise: Seven business innovators and the empires they built.* New York: HarperBusiness.

U.S. Census Bureau. (2001). *The statistical abstract of the United States.* Washington, DC: U.S. Government Printing Office.

Walstad, W.B., & Kourilsky, M.L. (1999). *Seeds of success: Entrepreneurship and youth.* Dubuque, IA: Kendall/Hunt Publishing.

Social Entrepreneurship edited by Marilyn L. Kourilsky and William B. Walstad
© *2003, Senate Hall Academic Publishing.*

5. Entrepreneurship in K-12 Public Education

Paul T. Hill
The University of Washington

Abstract. The thesis of this paper is that American public education is sorely hurt by false certainty, and that greater openness to entrepreneurship could lead to more adaptable and effective schools. Educators like to say "we know how to educate every child to high standards" but they then line up into opposing camps that struggle for control of schools via regulation. The keys to improvement in a field with technical uncertainty are provider discretion and performance accountability. If public education is to be more effective, especially for children who are not well served now, it must become open to entrepreneurship in four areas: providing support services, managing human resources, delivering complete courses, and operating whole schools.

Keywords: performance, accountability, privatization, entrepreneurship, regulation.

1. Democracy, Policy-Making, and Entrepreneurship

K-12 education is plagued by a lethal combination of weak technology and false certainty. Despite educators' claims to the contrary, we don't really know how to educate every child effectively, or even how to create large numbers of schools that work reasonably well for the vast numbers of children with "normal" needs and abilities. Though these are some schools that do this very well, no one has found a reliable way to reproduce them.

But because education is controlled by public policy, both educators and policymakers constantly search for the kind of general prescriptions that can be codified in law and regulation. Thus, educators and policymakers often endorse goals that no one knows how to attain and prescriptions that can't possibly have the positive effects claimed for them. For wildly unrealistic goals one need look no further than the National Education Goals established in 1989.[1]

These were dead letters the day they were established, in part because no one knew how to attain them and in part because their lead-times were too short even highly effective programs. For example, first the goal: "By the year 2000, the high school graduation rate will increase to at least 90 percent", and the related objective that "The gap in high school graduation rates between American students from minority backgrounds and their non-minority

---

1.   For complete information on the National Education goals see http//www.negp.gov.

counterparts will be eliminated" *were* unrealistic, in light of the fact that millions of members of the Class of 2000 had already reached the third grade without learning to read.

Twelve years later none of the education goals has been met, and it is debatable whether the scant progress made toward them can be validly measured.

More recently, all but two of the states have established standards for student learning in early grades, middle school, and high school. These purport to establish what every child needs to know and be able to do at a particular age: in theory a child who does not meet the standards will be unable to succeed at higher levels of education and ultimately be unprepared for productive work. But these standards have been created by political processes, usually featuring logrolling among groups of teacher committed to different subject matters. The result in many cases is standards that have no empirical basis: they might or might not be set too high, and students that fail to meet them might or might not be unable to succeed in college or find good jobs.

Goals and standards can be good things, especially when they call attention to big performance inequalities, e.g, between central city and suburban children, or between whites and Asians on one hand and blacks and Hispanics on the other. But when based on false certainty, they can cause confusion and misdirect effort.

The ill effects of false certainty are also evident in policies that prescribe particular methods of instruction. The struggles about whether to require or forbid the teaching of phonics, or whether to root out or promote programs of bilingual education, are prime examples. Competent reading teachers use a mixture of phonics and whole word approaches; none would ever consider using only phonics or no phonics. Similarly, effective schools teaching immigrant students use varying combinations of English and the students' native languages, whatever it takes to help students learn. Policies forbidding or mandating a practice reflect the balance of political forces at a particular time, not technical certainty.

Defenders of policy-driven K-12 education are prone to quote Churchill's dictum that "Democracy is the worst possible form of government except all the others that have been tried." However, the democracy they refer to is not an open system in which government is limited and individual freedom always gets the benefit of the doubt. Their version of democracy is a centralized deliberation leading to prescriptions that everyone must then obey. Some even glorify the fact that such deliberation can lead to coercive results, saying that it maintains education as a public space and ensures that all citizens will share certain formative experiences.[2]

Democracy might be the best system, but defining democracy as centralized deliberation leading to uniform coercive results is surely perverse. When controlled by policy, public education is defined by the relative strength of interest groups and their ability to control how issues are resolved in elections, legislatures, and courts. Policy reflects the interplay of adult interests, especially those of school employees and of parents who have intense views about their own children's education. Thus, education can be structured for the convenience of organized teachers, and activist parents can make sure the lion's share of money is spent on their own children. The bureaucracies created to implement policy also erect sharp boundaries between themselves and the rest of society, so that new ideas and interests have great difficulty getting a hearing.

These are the consequences of one strangely limited – if currently predominant – view of democracy. If seen more broadly, democracy is a system in which no individual or group is permanently excluded from influencing decisions and no issue is ever settled permanently. This is a Jeffersonian version of democracy, one that expects arrangements to be temporary, and institutions to be re-thought fundamentally as times and needs changed.

The latter form of democracy fits the realities of education. No process, whether deliberative or scientific, can validly prescribe a single solution for children from diverse needs; nor can it anticipate the skill requirements of a constantly changing society and economy. In education, only two things are certain: first, that not every child will learn best from the same form of instruction; and Second, that when today's children are adults they will need to know things that few if any members of their parents' generation know.

The best mechanism for coping with such uncertainty is entrepreneurship. As defined by Schumpeter, entrepreneurship is implementation of change via the introduction of new or better quality goods; new methods of production; new sources of supply; or reorganization of an industry. These are economic rather than political functions, but they can serve democracy, especially when there is so much uncertainty about how to accomplish a great goal, like effective public education.

The thesis of this paper is that American public education is sorely hurt by the lack of entrepreneurship, and that greater openness to entrepreneurship could make public education more adaptable and efficient.[3]

The paper has three parts: areas in which public education is weakened by being closed to entrepreneurship; how public education could be opened up to entrepreneurship; and what would be the greatest opportunities for education entrepreneurs.

---

2. See Gutmann, Amy and Dennis Thompson, *Democracy and Disagreement; Why Moral Conflict Cannot be Avoided in Politics, and What Should Be Done About It*. Cambridge MA, The Belknap Press of Harvard University Press, 1996, p.63-66.

3. Though entrepreneurship is usually inspired by the desire to make a profit, many potential entrepreneurs in education are nonprofits. These can become forces for innovation if the public school system will pay their costs and allow them to operate freely.

2. How the Lack of Entrepreneurship Weakens Public Education

A common observation among social service workers and foundations is that the public school system is the toughest and least malleable bureaucracy they deal with. Putting aside paramilitary organizations like police and fire departments, the public school system is the one city agency that most jealously guards entry into careers, most reverently follows its own rules, most suspiciously eyes outsiders offering to collaborate, and most carefully steers philanthropists and investors away from its own core functions.

Moreover, public education has little capacity to invest in new ideas. The vast preponderance of money in K-12 schools goes for salaries, and employment is controlled by certification rules and union contract provisions. Even when government increases education spending, union contract negotiations ensure that most of it is used for salary increases. Though there are substantial amounts of funds for teacher on-service training, the money is separated into small pots controlled by different federal and state programs. When there are new investments – e.g. California's recent major spending increase to reduce elementary school class size - there are targeted via policy.

These facts make it difficult for new ideas and new people to penetrate public education. Public schools allow small-scale innovation by individual teachers, but these are usually limited to one classroom or school. Not everyone in public education is happy with this situation, and there are many complaints about the futility of "random acts of innovation" and the impossibility of scaling up good ideas. There is no mechanism for a promising idea to capture a wider market, and no incentive for other teachers or schools to adopt a promising idea.

Becoming an unfriendly environment for entrepreneurship hurts public education in two ways: first, it is not able to adapt to changes in student demography and needs; and second, it can seldom take full advantage of ideas and resources available in the broader society.

With respect to student demography, anyone who studies big-city public school systems is award of schools whose population has been transformed by neighborhood turnover, from predominantly native English speakers to predominantly non-English speaking immigrants. In many localities these schools continue employing employ the same teachers, and the same methods, as before the population change occurred.

With respect to use of ideas available in the broader society, our cities are treasure houses filled with human talent and great institutions - museums and universities, orchestras, religious institutions and foundations, all of them dedicated to learning and to uplifting the human spirit. Unfortunately, the way we now run public education has kept these institutions on the sidelines. They can give money and moral support, but they cannot create or operate public schools, nor can their musicians, scientists, writers and artists teach students, except before and after school hours or as volunteers.

Some districts use help from "outside" sources like businesses, health clinics and arts institutions. However, these are generally used as supplementary resources rather than integrated into the basic instructional program.[4] Superintendents in districts where the school system has low technical capacity (e.g. Memphis and San Antonio) have purchased comprehensive staff training and instructional guidance programs from New American Schools, a nonprofit. However, these actions generated hot opposition and were ultimately reversed, largely because school board members and permanent central office bureaucrats resented spending "their" money on "outsiders".

This combination of inflexibility and distance from the rest of society gives many cities a much weaker and less effective public education system than they could have. Important functions are performed far more badly by public school systems than by most other long-lived American institutions, both non-profit and for-profit.[5] These include:

- Quality control: Careful assessment of the performance of individual schools or teachers, and intervention either to improve or replace them.

- Creation of new products: Creation of new schools to meet emerging needs and to provide options for children now in low-performing schools.

- Reaction to competition: Marshaling resources to upgrade low operations whose customers are unhappy and threatening to leave.

- Staff recruitment and career development: Recruiting the ablest people available and nurturing their capacities via carefully managed developments assignments.

- Financial control: Ensuring that costs of all activities are transparent and can be closely tracked, in support of program management and investment decisions.

---

4. See, for example, Celio, Mary Beth, *Random Acts of Kindness*, Seattle, Center on Re-Inventing Public Education, 1995.
5. I say long-lived in order to include the incompetent organizations and businesses that continually arise but are quickly destroyed by competition of lack of funding.

School districts are constrained from performing these functions by many things: union contract provisions that allocate teachers on the basis of seniority; senior teachers' tenure in particular schools; the beliefs that teachers are interchangeable and that schools are created only by assembling a sufficient number of teachers; teacher allocation rules that allow experienced teachers to avoid the most challenged schools, and guarantee that those schools will have constantly-shifting casts of inexperienced teachers; central office expenditure of all money; and functional accounting that makes it impossible to treat any unit – whether a central office bureau or a school – as a cost center.

The result is a system in which no one has significant discretion over who is hired, where they are assigned, or how money is spent. People who recognize new needs and have new ideas are regularly thwarted by the fact that the system is bound up in rules and customs. A few superintendents (e.g. Alan Bersin of San Diego) have recognized that entrepreneurship is possible only if dollars and jobs are managed more flexibly. However, as new studies of school district budgeting have shown, the forces for stasis are strong and have – at least to date – resisted the most determined efforts of reformist superintendents and school boards.

3. How Public Education Can Become Open to Entrepreneurship

The key to entrepreneurship is discretion. If entrepreneurs from outside or inside the system are to make a contribution to its performance, someone must be capable of making real choices and reallocating real money.

However, as the foregoing section shows, public school systems are structured to minimize discretion and to obscure the flow of money. The system is, moreover, structured in these ways for what some people consider good reasons. It minimizes the power of principals, so that teachers are not subject to arbitrary treatment, and it hides transactions that could be controversial, e.g. reductions in regular instruction to support costly placements for small numbers of handicapped children. Many people benefit from these attributes of the system; so opening public education to entrepreneurship will not be easy.

For years, people unhappy with the performance of public school systems have exhorted teachers and administrators to get outside the box, to innovate. However, experience has shown that exhortation and celebration of heroes does not change anything. The system tolerates a few zealots like celebrated school principal Debby Meier, and points to them as evidence of its flexibility and openness to change. But their initiatives remain scarce and short-lived.[6] The system also encourages philanthropists like Walter Annenberg, who gave hundreds of millions of dollars to support initiatives that school districts themselves could not pay for. Annenberg's money is now mostly spent, and though the initiatives he paid for were visible for a while, many have already faltered or disappeared.

There is no escaping the conclusion that public school systems can be fully open to entrepreneurship only if money that is now tied up can be released and reallocated. New public spending can encourage potential entrepreneurs, but entrepreneurship can flourish only if the anti-entrepreneurial features of the public education system are weakened. This requires change in policies and contracts, and also discipline on the part of entrepreneurs.

At the policy level, the most direct way to free up money is to eliminate any routine funding for central administrative units, and put all the money in schools, based on enrollment. Many current reform proposals are based on the idea that money should follow children to schools and that schools should then make the major purchasing decisions – what teachers to hire, how to mix teacher labor with use of technology, and what forms of advice and assistance to buy. This is one idea that unites the vouchers, charters, and school contracting movements.[7] All of them intend to make the flow of funds to schools transparent, and make sure that schools are free to buy what they need from a competitive marketplace of vendors. Under any of these proposals, school district bureaucracies might continue to exist, but only if voluntary fees paid by schools could sustain them.

Leaders of individual schools then will become entrepreneurs who commit to welldefined approaches to instruction and then assemble the necessary teachers, administrators, materials and links to Internet sites that provide learning materials and interactive experiences. Principals (or groups of teachers who form cooperatives to run schools) will attract students on the basis of quality instruction and demonstrated results. They will be funded, in effect, by families that choose to enroll students and therefore bring public dollars. School leaders and teachers will have strong incentives to cooperate with one another and to search constantly for better ways to promote student learning. Everyone's ability to keep a good and satisfying job will depend on the school's ability to maintain parents' confidence that it is the best possible option for the children served.

A less radical-sounding proposal, standards-based reform, could lead in the same direction. As adopted by all but 2 of the states, standards-based reform makes individual schools responsible for students' performance on

---

6. See Hess, Frederick, *Spinning Wheels*, Brookings 1999, about how many initiatives are tried at a small scale but abandoned before they spread. On the difficulties of resolving within-district financial inequities, see Roza, Marguerite and Karen Hawley-Miles, *A New Look at Inequities in School Funding: a Presentation on the Resource Variations within Districts*, Seattle, Center on Re-Inventing Public Education, 2002.
7. For a much more extended discussion of similarities and differences among these reform initiatives see Hill, Paul T. and Mary Beth Celio, *Fixing Urban Schools*, Washington D.C., The Brookings Press, 1998.

state tests. In return for accepting stringent new performance expectations, schools are supposed to gain control over funding, spending, hiring, use of time, and selection of instructional methods. If these commitments were kept, schools would have the same kind of financial discretion sought by vouchers, chartering, and school contracting proposals. Though all major elements of the public education establishment once endorsed standards-based reform, the pro-standards coalition is now fraying badly, as teachers unite in opposition to standards-based tests and administrators balk at relinquishing control of funds. It is still possible, however, that standards-based reform will ultimately free up some funding and create some room for entrepreneurship.

People who believe in the power of entrepreneurship, or who want to be entrepreneurs themselves, must recognize the importance of policy change. In the past, some business leaders have opposed money-follows-the-child proposals, arguing that big sales of millions of dollars worth of computers or books are possible only if decisions are centralized. However, as these businesses have found, the decisions of politically controlled school systems shift with election results and have little to do with the relative merits of products.[8] Though a few firms can make money selling to big centralized school districts, most will remain limited, as now, to administrative and supplementary services. Public education will not be fully open to entrepreneurship until spending is in the hands of people who manage individual schools and take responsibility for students' results.

Entrepreneurs can, however, advance their own cause by developing products and services that schools, as they gain control of critical decisions, will need. The next section suggests what those products and services will be.

4. The Most Promising Areas for Entrepreneurship

Because few aspects of public K-12 education have been subject to competition or cost control, it is likely that virtually every function could be done more efficiently. Some functions are demanding, however, and it is not clear that "turning it all over to the private sector" could lead to lead to prompt improvements. It is also unlikely that entrepreneurs would be completely free to pursue every alternative that might look more effective or less costly. As voucher proponent Terry Moe argues so convincingly, K-12, education will always be subject to some regulation and public oversight.[9]

---

8.   Recently, New American Schools has determined that its school designs cannot be prooerly implemented in districts that retain central control over schools' funding, staffing, use of time, and selection of instructional materials. See Berends, Mark, Susan J. Bodilly, Sheila Nataraj Kirby, *Facing the Challenges of Whole-School Reform. New American Schools After a Decade*, Santa Monica, RAND 2002.

However, if the laws governing public education are changed to allow money to follow children and individual schools to make spending decisions, many important opportunities for entrepreneurial innovation will arise. These will be of four kinds:

• Providing support services

• Managing human resources

• Delivering complete courses

• Operating whole schools

This section will provide examples of entrepreneurial opportunities in each of these categories.

4.1. Providing Support Services

Private enterprises already provide bus transportation and food service in many school districts, and property maintenance service in a few. These are significant activities, but they do not control as much money or influence instruction as much as other services that entrepreneurs might offer, including:

Creation of local real estate investment trusts to own, develop, sell, purchase, and lease school facilities. This is a remedy for one of the costliest inefficiencies plaguing school districts: they own many buildings that are outmoded, costly to operate, and in the wrong place. The mission of such a trust would be to ensure that all publicly funded schools (traditional schools, charter schools, and contract schools) have timely access to the space they need. A trust would have the freedom and incentive to use a variety of tools to make sure every publicly funded school has a decent facility. It might allow other community organizations to rent space while schools are not in session – so-called mixed-use agreements – in order to squeeze some of the market value out of school properties.[10] It might also enter partnerships to take advantage of private providers' capital-raising advantages.

---

9. Moe, Terry M., "The Structure of Choice," in Paul T. Hill, ed., *Choice With Equity*, Stanford, Hoover Institution Press, 2002.
10. Most districts have under-used school buildings in the wrong place, and overcrowded schools elsewhere. Innovation Partners in Portland is developing an independent real estate trust that manages, leases out, and redevelops existing school buildings and either builds or rents others. They are also moving toward private development of school facilities that can easily be remodeled, e.g to accommodate smaller or larger class sizes, more intense use of technology, or even rental to businesses.

Underwriting insurance to pay for schools' special education liabilities. This is a remedy for uncontrolled growth of special education costs, drawing funds away from regular classroom instruction. Underwriters could cover schools in the event students needed expensive special services. Schools could eventually be loss-rated, so that fee structures would encourage schools to use expensive special services only when absolutely necessary. Handicapped children would benefit, since insurance would guarantee funding for services when they were truly needed.

4.2. Managing Human Resources

This is a "core" function that districts normally keep inside. However, district human resource departments do not serve schools: instead, they administer district policy and ensure that personnel allocation is consistent with seniority rights and other union contract provisions. If schools were free to hire teachers and other staff, they would need vendors that could find the kinds of teachers they needed and provide payroll services and benefits packages. Opportunities for entrepreneurs could include:

"Head hunting" to find teachers who fit individual schools. This is a common private sector function, and one that many private schools use. But school district personnel offices do not perform it. Firms that built long-term relationships with individual schools could make reasonable incomes and contribute to maintenance of good schools.

Developing new sources of teachers. Science, mathematics, special education, and other teachers with rare skills could be employed by independent organizations, which would be manpower vendors, providing teachers on a contract basis. Such organizations could employ teachers and provide their salaries and benefits. Individual schools would contract with them for instructional services; the amounts paid could combine current salaries, benefits, and expenditures for in-service training and substitutes. The providers would then be responsible for recruitment, training, and compensation. As contract employees, teachers would not be covered by the same rules on pay and certification that now constrain school districts.

Providing portable employee benefits. Current teacher retirement funds are tied to particular school systems or states, and subject to benefit limits that discourage senior teachers from working past their mid-50s. Inflexible government benefit packages also give teachers less freedom than private sector employees to select among health insurance, housing assistance, and other benefits providers. Current benefits for teachers are typically good for married, settled middle-aged people, but less valuable for younger, single, mobile people. Privately managed, portable retirement funds would expand the pool of potential teachers in two ways. First, they would allow people to move more readily from private sector jobs into teaching, and vice versa. Second, privately-managed portable retirement funds would ease the problem of "maxing out". This common provision of government retirement plans means that senior employees eventually reach a point at which they cannot add further to their retirement savings. Understanding that their real incomes have suddenly dropped sharply, many leave public employment at about age 55. More flexible benefits plans could solve this system and thereby reduce premature teacher retirements.

4.3. Delivering Complete Courses

Though vendors often provide books, filmstrips, and other materials used in instruction, teachers then use these items. The use of materials, and the coherency of overall presentation, remains with the teacher. The teacher's salary is also the most expensive part of any instructional package. However, there are some subjects that few teachers are qualified to integrate well. The result is that mathematics above basic algebra, laboratory sciences, and advanced language courses are taught poorly – and in some localities, not at all.

Providing such coursework on-line, whether via programmed instruction or interaction between students and an expert instructor, is a major entrepreneurial opportunity. Microsoft cofounder Paul Allen's company APEX is creating on-line courses for high school AP (advanced placement) courses. However, there is still room for regular mathematics, science, and language classes, at the junior and senior high levels. These could be sold to schools that cannot find qualified teachers, or that prefer to use teachers as seminar leaders or British-style tutors.

4.4. Operating Whole Schools

Big city school districts often struggle to transform schools that have failed generations of children. The efforts districts are capable of – re-training of teachers, replacement of principals, and "reconstitution" of teaching forces – seldom work, for several reasons. Teachers in the lowest performing schools leave those schools as soon as they schools as they gain even a year's seniority and can claim a job elsewhere. Training they receive while working in a failed school equips them to work in their next assignment; meanwhile the failed school receives another batch of green, poorly prepared teachers. Principal replacement can make a big difference, if the district can find an excellent principal willing to take on a risky and difficult job. On average, new principals are no better able to cope with failed schools than the people they replace. Finally, district-managed reconstitution does not make a school more attractive to teachers or administrators. Thus, the new post-reconstitution staff is seldom any more skillful or capable of strategic action than the group they replaced.

By hiring independent organizations to take over failed schools, district leaders hope to gain many advantages: an independent group can start with a definite approach to instruction, and can hire teachers and administrators who understand and want to follow that approach. Edison is the best-known school provider; its curriculum and teaching methods are well known, and it can search nationally for school staff that want to work in a particular way. Edison also trains teachers and principals in its methods, and exercises some quality control over school processes and performance. Other smaller for-profits following similar business models include Mosaica, and Advantage Schools. A growing number of non-profits (e.g. Aspire and KIPP schools) are offering similar services.

School providers are finding this a tough business, in part because districts seldom give the operator full control of the school. Edison, for example, has accepted some contracts that require it to hire the same teacher union members who worked in the schools before Edison took responsibility for them. For-profit operators also encounter ideological opposition from community activists who distrust business. As this is written, ideological opposition to Edison, as the largest and most visible for-profit, has led to dramatic declines in the company's stock price and might threaten its existence.[11] [12]

Independent school providers also contract with community groups that have received charters to operate individual schools. Charters give the school operator greater freedom on hiring, hours of operation, and pay scales. However, many of the community groups that hire school providers are fractious and inexperienced. As Edison has found, these small governing boards can micromanage and disrupt the instructional program.

Despite these troubles, school operation is and extremely important entrepreneurial Opportunity. It can allow independent providers to use school time in ways forbidden by district teacher contracts, and it can reward providers that combine teacher work and technology in innovative ways. The school provider that becomes a good "systems integrator", using technology-

---

11. The wave of ideologically driven opposition to Edison has crested in three cities, San Francisco, New York, and Philadelphia. In each city the company was portrayed as a carpetbagger taking money that should be controlled locally. ACORN, a leftist community action group with chapters in many cities, has also made headlines by portraying Edison as a white organization that can victimize Black children. This is so despite the fact that many Edison top managers are African-Americans.
12. Ideological opposition is not the only threat to Edison's stock price. The company has also been criticized by the Securities and Exchange Commission for overstating earnings.

based instruction well and focusing teacher work on tutoring and diagnosis, can become a low-cost, high-performance provider.

The need for new school providers is still strong. In the course of a recent state takeover, Philadelphia's hiring of such organizations was limited only by the supply. There are not enough whole-school operators to meet the needs of one big city. State and federal laws are now in place that could require dozens of cities to hire operators for large numbers of schools.

Edison's experience has convinced many investors that non-profit school operators are more likely to succeed. However, successful school operation requires capital to devise and test instructional methods and create hiring, training, and quality control capacities. Some of the invests can come from philanthropy, but profit-seeking investors are also needed. Smaller forprofit operators – with less flamboyant management – might be far less newsworthy and therefore more viable.

Some critics have suggested that Edison and other for-profit providers are struggling in part because their schools are not very distinctive. This is possibly true; most for-profit providers use off the shelf curricula and training program that school districts themselves can buy. (Edison, for example, uses John Hopkins University's "Success For All Reading"). Some school districts have cancelled their contracts with such providers, claiming they can run the same programs themselves. Truly successful for-profit whole-school providers will probably need to develop proprietary methods, including novel uses of technology for core instruction, that cannot be readily imitated.

5. Conclusion

For decades, public education has been frozen by laws, regulations, and labor contracts. Money is tied up in many unproductive uses – e.g. unneeded buildings, inefficient central offices, teaching forces not disciplined by performance pressures. Entrepreneurship is needed in every aspect of school and system operations. But it is not easy. As we have already seen, "the private sector" might, but does not always, find ways to increase efficiency. Entrepreneurs who recognize the potential for improvement in public education, but also know that the work is hard and demanding, can make a difference, especially in those places where public education now performs most badly.

6. Potential of For-Profit Schools for Educational Reform

Henry M. Levin [1]

Columbia University

Abstract. The rise of a for-profit industry in elementary and secondary schools is a relatively recent phenomenon in American education. In the past, a small number of independent schools – probably 2 percent or less – were for-profit endeavors, usually owned by a family or a small group of educators. However, over the last decade a group of for-profit firms has emerged with the goal of managing public schools on a contract basis. These firms have established contracts with both charter schools and public school districts. In exchange for a per-student fee (often the average per-student expenditure in a district or the amount of charter school reimbursement from the state), they will manage both the logistical and instructional aspects of the school. These firms can be analyzed according to their ability: (1) to be adequately profitable to attract capital; and (2) to improve education and initiate reforms in their schools, and stimulate reform in other schools that face competition from them or wish to emulate them. This paper suggests that the ability of EMOs (Educational Management Organizations) to be profitable is, at best, problematic. Although spokespersons for almost all EMOs suggest that it is only a matter of gaining more schools to reach economies of scale, the evidence on scale economies in education is at odds with this claim. A combination of high cost structures at central headquarters and the need for major marketing activities are also major challenges. In addition, education is a much tougher business than many of the EMOs anticipated because of the many-layers of political scrutiny and the ability of charter school sponsors and school districts to cancel term contracts after relative short periods. On the basis of existing evidence we have not yet seen substantial innovation in instruction by for-profit EMOs, although we have seen some logistical advantages in school organization. Evidence on educational outcomes is also mixed. This paper concludes with the view that for-profit EMOs are less promising than potential other forms of for-profit endeavors in education.

Keywords: for-profit schools, education reform, educational privatization, school efficiency.

1. Introduction

Private schools preceded public schools in American history. Although schooling was often a cottage industry in colonial times in which an adult might provide tutoring for a fee to one or more students in a household, private schools as organized institutions were not designed to yield profits. School

---

1.   The author is Director of the National Center for the Study of Privatization in Education and the William Heard Kilpatrick Professor of Economics and Education, Teachers College, Columbia University. He wishes to thank his colleagues Clive Belfield and Janelle Scott for their reviews and suggestions. The author may be reached at hl361@columbia.edu.

organizations were likely to be church-affiliated and dedicated to particular educational, philosophical, and religious values. Only at the beginning of the nineteenth century do we see the rise of what was ultimately to be called the common or public school as each of the states adopted education as a constitutional responsibility.

Towards the end of the nineteenth century, a system of Catholic schools was established to shield Catholic students from the Protestant bias found in public schools and to provide religious instruction (Tyack 1974: 84-86). In terms of sheer numbers of schools and enrollments, the Catholic schools soon outnumbered the other independent schools in enrollments, as they do today. At the same time, public schooling continued to expand, and by the turn of the twentieth century almost all states had compulsory attendance laws. A major controversy arose over whether independent or private schools could meet compulsory attendance requirements. This issue was resolved by the U.S. Supreme Court in 1925 in Pierce vs Society of Sisters which declared that compulsory schooling laws could be met in any independent school approved by the state.

What is notable in this brief historical flow is the absence of a significant presence of for-profit schools in the development of the U.S. educational system. This raises the question of whether there is something about education that does not lend itself well to for-profit operations (Levin 2001). There are undoubtedly a relatively small number of family-run schools or those operated by individuals or partnerships that provide a living to these families or individuals. However, even these are not common, and there is little evidence of substantial returns on investment. In general, long hours and constant attention to a specific clientele seem to be needed to make these schools succeed, an experience that is also common in privately-run pre-schools.

The last decade has seen the rise of for-profit companies in elementary and secondary education, but few of them own schools. Rather, they have established businesses for contracting with school districts or charter schools to operate their schools, functioning as educational management organizations or EMO's. These schools continue to function as public schools even though they are run by private contractors. Charter schools are a relatively recent phenomenon (Cookson & Berger 2002; Finn, Manno, & Vanourek 2000; Murphy & Shiffman 2002). Such schools are given both specified public funding and dispensation from most state and local rules and regulations in order to provide greater autonomy in operations. In order to qualify as a charter school they must tender an application to the charter school authorities in their state (typically school districts, universities, or state departments of education) with a clear purpose (charter) that they will address and the enrollment objectives, organization, staffing, and provisions for financial accountability. Many groups establishing charter schools have had little or no experience in operating schools, so they have sought assistance. Thus, it is hardly a surprise that the growth of EMOs has followed closely the growth of charter schools in the U.S., of which there are about 2,400 in 2002 in 37 states and the District of Columbia enrolling some 600,000 students.[2] Most charter schools are "start-ups", that is newly established schools; but some are conversions of existing public schools to charter status. Reinforcing this link, charter schools also turn to EMOs because charter funding structures tend to disadvantage schools that do not have access to capital funds. EMOs may provide access to start-up capital.

In addition, EMOs have been active in contracting with school districts to operate specific schools within those districts, usually schools with poor educational results and many challenges. The district provides a specified amount of funding, often a generous arrangement for the EMO relative to the funding provided to comparable schools operated by the district.[3] In some cases the EMOs have been able to get additional funding from philanthropic organizations because of their commitment to school reform. One advantage of contracting directly with school districts is the availability of a school facility, an advantage also conferred upon some charter school conversions. In contrast, the establishment of new charter schools requires a search for and financing of a proper facility – and many states do not provide funding or adequate funding to pay for charter school facilities.

It is appropriate to examine whether for-profit EMOs have the potential to reform public education. To answer that question one must ask two further questions. First, can EMOs succeed as a business, and under what conditions? Second, are EMOs likely to stimulate changes in elementary and secondary schools that will improve educational outcomes. Clearly, if EMOs are not adequately profitable, they are unlikely to have an educational impact in the long run. Even if they prosper, the next question is whether they will change education through innovation and competition.

2. Can For-Profit EMOs Be Profitable?

It is useful to begin by setting out the early expectations of both the founders of EMOs and the investment community as to why this looked like a promising opportunity. In the early 1990s, the climate for privatizing public services had been well-established. The Reagan and Bush administrations had criticized government as the problem rather than the solution and had praised the private

---

2. The Center for Educational Reform provides a continuous update of schools and enrollments. See http://www.edreform.com.
3. A common arrangement is to provide the average per-student expenditure of the district even though the district average includes services not provided by the contracted school. See Levin (1998: 383-384) and Miron & Nelson (2002: 62-68) on the cost accounting issues when comparing the costs of public versus private schools.

sector, deregulation, and tax reduction as the solution to inadequate public services. The Clinton and Gore administration followed up this appeal with a variety of approaches to Reinventing Government, including privatization of government services and continued support for privatization of health care through Health Maintenance Organizations (HMOs).

The specific appeal to the investment community for privatizing elementary and secondary education was a sector spending almost one billion dollars a day, the largest government sector that had been untouched by privatization. Wall Street firms went to their investment communities with glossy presentations showing declines in test scores, poor test results relative to those in other countries, rising educational expenditure, and particular educational challenges in the inner cities (e.g. Merrill Lynch, 1999). Many of these critiques were overstated, and the causes of the shortcomings were overly-simplified as being the fruits of leaving education to government bureaucracies. In short, it was asserted that funding was spent inefficiently with too little being allocated to classrooms and too much to central administrative headquarters of school districts. Educational specialists in the investment industry argued that if the education sector were privatized, its performance would rise, and the returns to investors would be substantial because of the enormous gains in efficiency. Indeed, such investments were referred to as opportunities to do well (high returns) by doing good (improving education), so they were both economically and morally justified.

This wave of justification for privatization had one major down-side. Few of those who decided to enter the business of education had studied carefully the economics or politics of education. They failed to look carefully at resource allocation in existing public schools and its underlying justification, primarily in the belief that whatever was being done was highly inefficient and could be easily improved by the private sector. They assumed that there were large economies of scale in running schools so that profitability would be an increasing function of size of firm and the numbers of schools managed. They did not understand the politics of education and the fact that when public dollars are financing the enterprise it cannot be separated from political decision-making. At a time when large fortunes were made on selling possibilities and dreams, due-diligence was in short supply in the new economy.

What they did not realize is: (1) education is a tough business because it is regulated, monitored, and subject to the demands of multiple audiences and layers of government on the basis of public funding; (2) EMOs are challenged by high marketing costs that public schools do not face; (3) relatively short-term contracts (3-5 years) have their own risks in amortizing investments at school sites – whether the EMO does well or poorly; (4) the economies of scale that were anticipated do not exist; and (5) one size does not fit all, creating a challenge for a uniform educational model, quality control from afar, and the establishment of national and regional brands.

3. Education is a Tough Business

Ideally, a business would like to provide a concrete product or service with as few restrictions as possible and delivered under stable conditions to a predictable clientele. Risk, change, and uncertainty are unwelcome and require a premium in returns. As Cyrus Driver has found in applying contract theory to school administration, education is characterized by multiple goals and authorities with constant shifts in the relative importance among each as political, demographic, and social trends intervene. Multiple goals include establishing schools as safe and disciplined environments accommodating a wide variety of student needs, ranging from those of gifted students to those of handicapped students. Goals include developing student skills in a multitude of subjects including reading, writing, speaking, mathematics, science, social studies, art, foreign languages, and physical capacities. They also include development of creativity, character (such as respect, honesty, judgment, and persistence), problem-solving, personal health and hygiene, patriotism, and citizenship. From the standpoint of a productive enterprise, this is a complicated production process because it is one in which many "products" must be produced simultaneously and with limited resources that require continuous tradeoffs among goals. Furthermore, student capabilities, motivations, and goals have a profound influence on educational outcomes, factors that are often beyond the control of schools.

Schools are subject to the interventions and pressures of three government bodies and the demands of their clientele. For example, contracted schools within school districts are governed by federal, state, and local laws, regulations, and policies. These strictures and guidelines are voluminous and often difficult to interpret or understand because of their multitudinous details and complexity. The recently passed federal law, <u>No Child Left Behind</u>, is more than one thousand pages, a single law among tens of thousands. It will be translated into concrete procedures and regulations by federal agencies for transmission to the states; each state will interpret these details and apply them to local districts, providing hundreds of new regulations and thousands of pages of interpretation for school authorities. Definitions of allowable achievement tests, testing frequency and procedures, and the consequences of tests for students and schools will be determined for all schools including charter schools. Three levels of government monitor contract schools in each district. State chartering agencies monitor charter schools according to federal regulations and to those state regulations that have not been relaxed.

In addition, the clientele and potential clientele for these schools provide pressure in a variety of ways. For charter schools, families have the prerogative of choice and will leave if they believe that the charter school has not delivered what they want. In addition, they have access to the charter school board, charter school director, and individual staff to press for the types of services they want for their children. Schools contracting with EMOs within school districts face similar pressures from parents and through the various governing mechanisms. Finally, teacher and other professional organizations often set restrictions on hiring and working conditions based upon either their collective bargaining agreements or their political power.

The result of all of the government regulation and scrutiny and that of the choice options and demands of clientele is that the EMO is subject to competing pressures and changes from many sides, with little stability over time. It must somehow find a way to balance a large number of competing claims, a phenomenon that does not lend itself well to a standard schooling process that will allow substantial uniformity across different sites. Yet, most of the EMOs seek to establish national and regional brands that promote a uniform model, one that is highly consistent from site-to-site and confers a brand image.

4. Marketing and Contracting Costs

EMO's face costs that do not have to be borne by local school districts. The most important are the marketing costs that are required to attract and sign charter schools and districts to contracts. Not only are the EMOs competing against other EMOs, but there is overall resistance by many citizens and educators to delegating schools to for-profit management. To many, the disagreement is fundamental, the view that profits will come from squeezing services rather than from greater efficiency. They believe that such schools have incentives to select students who will be least problematic and require few services outside of routinized instruction, leaving the more costly student needs to the regular public schools. The result is that EMOs must engage in substantial promotion and marketing activities, from advertising to participating in the regional and national conventions of education associations, and also to direct marketing of the EMO concept and services to school districts. The last of these may consist of direct appeals to administrators and school boards through expensive retreats at which the potential decision-makers are provided with luxury accommodations, meals, and entertainment, as well as presentations by the sponsoring EMO.

Marketing activity requires substantial personnel who solicit school districts and potential charter school organizers or even offer to do all of the preparation of applying for charter school status. For every contract that is obtained, the EMO may have to solicit intensively among a much larger number of potential districts or charter school sponsors. Even when there is overall agreement on establishing a contractual relation, the details must be worked out by lawyers, accountants, and business executives on the EMO staff to assure that the EMO obtains a beneficial contract. Both the marketing and contracting costs must be funded ultimately from the operational revenues received from states or school districts, excess expenses that are not intrinsic to school districts that operate their own schools.

5. Short-Term Contracts

Typical contracts between EMOs and charter schools or school districts are only three to five years. This means that overhead costs for establishing the contract and gearing up to operate the school must be amortized over a relatively short period of time, especially given the risks of contract non-renewal. Contracts may not be renewed for poor performance, and many argue that it takes at least five years to turn around a failing school or to get a new charter school on its feet. This means that the EMO risks losing contracts before it can amortize appropriately its start-up expenses. But, the situation is also precarious if the EMO succeeds. It is clear that districts seek for-profit EMOs to operate schools that are dysfunctional and performing poorly, not its better schools. Often these dysfunctional schools have poor leadership, unqualified teachers, disruptive students, high pupil mobility, and community factionalism. If the EMO is able to turn around the school in five years to make it functional, the school district may have an incentive to take the school back into its own operational fold.[4]

6. Elusive Economies of Scale

Among the most seriously erroneous assumptions built into the business models was that there are substantial economies of scale in education (e.g. Chubb 2001). The thinking seemed to go something like this. The establishment of a for-profit company will entail a large fixed expenditure for addressing all of the above issues and more. But, the amount that will be received for each student will allow a fairly large surplus of revenues over costs for operations at the school site. The logic seemed to be that there is considerable waste at the school site in conventional public schools, although where substantial savings might be made was never specifically identified. As

---

4. There is some evidence of this phenomenon in the recent announcement by the charter school's board that it would take over the Renaissance School from Edison Schools.

in the appeals to investors, the assumption of greater efficiency of the private sector was used to justify this claim. In order to offset the high fixed costs of a central headquarters, it was only necessary to contract with enough schools. In this way the high fixed costs would be spread over enough schools that a net profit would be generated from school operations.

This meant that the high costs of getting started and establishing EMOs were to be expected, with attendant losses over the early period, and it justified large amounts of investment capital prior to profitability. But, the business model suffered from one major flaw. Not only had no one demonstrated the economies of scale that were counted on, but the economics of education literature finds that economies of scale set in at fairly low enrollments at both school sites and in school districts. Many EMOs have already expanded far beyond the most efficient scale in terms of enrollments. The reason is that schools have very high variable costs. Each new school requires a facility; administrators, teaching and support staff; equipment and supplies; maintenance; utilities; and other resources. Since schools are labor intensive, virtually the only way to reduce costs substantially is to use lower-cost staffing and labor-saving technology. But, teachers and educational administrators are not highly paid relative to their responsibilities and to other professional groups, so savings are limited by a restrictive teacher supply at lower remuneration. Further, parents and state regulations oppose cutting back educational qualifications to substitute less-skilled labor for professionals. And, educational technology has historically represented added cost at school sites – without assurance of educational benefits – rather than a guaranteed strategy for capital-labor substitution (Cuban 2001).

To reduce costs at school sites, the EMOs have pursued three strategies. The first is to try to save costs by hiring less experienced teachers. The problem with this strategy is that younger teachers are more likely to leave to start families, return to college, seek better positions, or accommodate changes in the career of a spouse. This turnover creates additional costs for recruitment and training, and these may offset completely the salary advantage. The second is to use standard operating[5] procedures and low-cost educational strategies that minimize the need for ancillary personnel and provide a bare-bones pedagogy in which all teachers follow a standard script of instruction at each grade level. This approach also has costs in terms of mobility of teachers who seek more creative opportunities, as well as the further challenge that one approach may not fit all students at all sites. In addition, such approaches with

---

5. In the latest review of the evidence on economies of scale, the authors conclude that: "Sizable potential cost savings may exist by moving from a very small district (500 or less pupils) to a district with ca 2000-4000 pupils, both in instructional and administrative costs. Per pupil costs may continue to decline slightly until an enrollment of roughly 6,000, when diseconomies of scale start to set in (Andrews, Duncombe, and Yinger 2002):255)".

their emphasis on basic skills may not be appropriate to the increasing sophistication of tests to measure higher order skills and creativity.

The third strategy for reducing costs is to recruit and retain students who are least demanding in terms of resources. It is no surprise that most EMOs do not accommodate moderate or severely handicapped students, but they can also discourage students with even modest behavioral problems or learning needs. Or they can maintain strict requirements on parental participation, discouraging single parent families and those who face difficulties in taking on additional responsibilities. Strict discipline policies can be used to suspend or expel disruptive students. In the long run scrutiny by local and state education agencies and by communities will create resistance to these policies as well as undermining public relations.

Overall, the strategy of large-scale expansion before becoming profitable is not a promising one, based upon three decades of research on economies of scale. The most recent summary of research on the topic (Andrews, Duncombe, and Younger 2002) finds that the lowest average cost per student is reached with a school district enrolling about 6,000 students. The largest of the EMOs, Edison Schools had about 130 schools and 75,000 students in the Spring of 2002. Yet it suffered $ 17 million in losses in its most recent quarter (March 31, 2002) and cumulative losses since its founding in the early nineties of about $ 200 million. It continued to premise its future on a large expansion that would provide profitability based upon economies of scale, as have other EMOs. Yet, its present size is more than ten times the estimated size for an efficient school district. Moreover, there is considerable evidence that the average cost per student of larger districts rise considerably as supervision, monitoring, and communication become less efficient and require more personnel relative to enrollments. Even this evidence refers to a single school district. When one considers the long supply and communication lines when schools are spread over many districts and large regions, the added costs of maintaining such a large network are even higher than when concentrated in a single school district.

7. A Uniform Product

The business plans of the EMOs push for a uniform educational product across their school sites for several reasons. First, they seek to control costs by standardizing their use of curriculum, pedagogy, and school inputs. A standard approach provides several advantages. First, it means that the procedures for establishing and operating schools, selecting and training personnel, and purchasing equipment and supplies can be routinized and made uniform throughout the enterprise and the school network that it sponsors. Personnel can be shifted among sites almost without disruption because of their commitment to and familiarity with a single operation. Moreover, to the degree that it obtains a common set of equipment and supplies for each school, it can benefit from competitive bidding and discounts for large purchases (even though such cost savings will be a modest part of the overall cost structure). Second, the uniformity of the educational product contributes to the notion of a recognized brand of education for a particular company. With national or regional aspirations, each EMO seeks to establish brand identity based upon product differentiation.

But, educational needs can differ immensely from one community to another. In some cases a majority of students are immigrants speaking a first language that is not English. Differences in home backgrounds, handicaps, giftedness, ethnicity, poverty, and cultures can create large variance in the types of educational programs and materials that will benefit particular groups of students. Differences in local customs with respect to educational organization can also be important. The states and school districts also set different criteria among subjects to be taught and tested, so adjustments must be made to meet these "standards". Further, demographic characteristics of students and educational content standards and testing programs change over time, sometimes very rapidly. All of these factors contradict the assumption that a standard model, representing a branded approach that changes little from site-to-site or over-time, is a sound business goal.

8. A Viable Business Model

It is highly dubious that the business model that has been pursued by many of the EMOs is viable economically. It appears that it is based more upon generic assumptions of greater business efficiency than a careful study of the specific features of school operations. Virtually all of these assumptions violate what is known about the economics and politics of schools. Schools must deal with multiple governments with conflicting priorities and constantly shifting objectives rather than a stable business context. EMOs face large costs of marketing and promotion and costs of contracting that do not seem to have been anticipated. The relatively short-term contracts that the EMOs are able to obtain do not allow sufficient time to amortize investments at school sites if contract renewals are not forthcoming. The substantial economies of scale that were anticipated in operations are illusory. And, the notion of a uniform model that can be implanted anywhere under a specific EMO brand does not comport with the reality of the different educational conditions encountered.

Although several of the EMOs have tried to make some adaptation over time, most have held to models largely based upon these fallacious assumptions. The result is that large operating losses have been continuing, and several have been unable to get continuous access to capital to finance their operations and cover their losses (e.g. Advantage Schools, Learn Now, Tesseract/EAI) and have gone out of business or merged with others. At this point the viability of the predominant model for privatizing schools, that of the EMO, seems highly dubious.[6]

It is difficult to attribute these poor results to inadequate financial remuneration. In the case of charter schools the EMOs are working with contracts based upon the same remuneration as the non-EMO charter schools, where most of the latter are able to succeed. Moreover, some of the charter schools using EMOs have been very successful in obtaining philanthropic contributions, as have some of the EMOs directly. Further, a common practice of the EMOs with respect to contracts with districts is to obtain a contract based upon a full share of the average per-student expenditure.[7] But, most of the contract schools do not provide the full range of central office services that the district must carry. Moreover, the contract schools are typically at the less-expensive elementary level rather than the more resource intensive secondary level; and the contract schools and charter schools operated by EMO's enroll few of the costly special education students, the moderately and severely handicapped. Thus, the contractual payments typically exceed what a comparable district school receives in resources.

9. Do EMOs Contribute to Educational Reform?

Even if the existing business models of the EMOs do not suggest economic viability, one can still examine their educational approaches to ask if they contribute to educational reform. There are two paths by which EMOs could stimulate educational reform. The first is to operate schools that make organizational or pedagogical breakthroughs that might lead to their success and to emulation by public schools. The second is to create competition between EMOs and public schools that will stimulate public schools to improve their operations. It is also possible that just the potential threat of EMOs, as opposed to direct competition, will spur the public schools to be more responsive to their clientele.

No careful survey has been made of the strategies of the EMOs, but descriptions of their approaches are found in promotional materials. In addition, there have been studies of particular schools (e.g. Miron & Nelson

---

6. There is a great deal of focus on when EMOs might reach the break-even point as if that is the criterion of success. But, the real issue is whether they can earn a substantial return on capital that will be competitive with other investment opportunities.

7. For a discussion of how to compare costs and the findings that suggest greater largesse received by EMOs than comparable school sites, see Miron and Nelson (2002: 62-68). For cost comparisons in Baltimore under an EMO that operated nine schools, see Richards, Shore, & Sawicky (1996: Chap. 2).

2002). I have also visited a small number. So, what follows is based upon a variety of sources, but not a systematic survey.

10. Pedagogical Approaches

There is little evidence of major new pedagogical approaches practiced by EMOs. Many EMOs emphasize a back-to-basics approach that is heavy on traditional drill and practice or what is called direct instruction. There are at least three reasons for reliance on this traditional approach. The first is that there is at least some evidence that direct instruction provides achievement gains in basic skills. Second, many school districts that are contracting with EMOs or charter schools are seeking traditional approaches and test score gains in basic skills. And, third, this approach keeps down costs for the EMOs because it is truly a no-frills method without enrichment and often with minimal instruction in the arts or areas outside of basic skills. The Edison Schools, the largest of the EMOs, rely largely upon standard curricula that can be purchased by any school district, although it has developed some applications for its technology and has incorporated other subjects. Edison relies heavily on a combination of direct instruction and broader approaches. Many of the other EMOs rely upon a "cookie-cutter" approach to the 3 Rs (Miron & Nelson 2002).

Without question there is no evidence of "revolutionary" breakthroughs by EMOs with respect to curriculum, instructional strategies, or use of technologies. Virtually every aspect of their pedagogical approaches can be found somewhere in existing public schools, and, in many cases, in a large number of public schools. Perhaps it is too early to expect these kinds of innovations or the funding is not adequate to create the incentives and development that are needed.[8]

11. Personnel and Organization

In the areas of personnel and organization, one finds definite departures from many existing public schools. In particular, many of the EMOs seem to do a more systematic job than the average public school in creating an overall system of personnel selection and training and curriculum consistency across the entire school. According to my observations and inquiries, the EMOs place more effort on selecting their school-site administrators and teaching personnel and evaluating both. In some cases they also provide more training

---

8.   Brown (1992) provides an economic analysis of why private schools deviate so little from
      public schools in their basic features.

and greater performance incentives. There is greater focus on accountability of site administrators and school staff through sanctions and rewards. The EMOs view schools as a system to a greater degree than I have seen in public schools where the pieces often lack coordination and "new" approaches are adopted helter-skelter.

This difference is especially notable in some of the inner-city environments where traditional public schools are chaotic with high teacher and administrator turnover, high student mobility, frequent shifts in curriculum approaches and pedagogies, uncoordinated staff development, and haphazard use of educational technologies. Even the appearance of the facility is unkempt and in need of repairs and renovations. In contrast the EMOs have a good record of attempting to select staff and immerse them in a more systematic pedagogical approach with articulation from grade to grade. Staff are evaluated on their success in implementing the curriculum and pedagogy and on student success, to the degree that it is possible to measure the latter.

Perhaps the greatest visible strength is the ability to of EMOs to accomplish the logistics of school maintenance. In many cases, the EMOs are able to physically transform school facilities that have been unsightly, damaged, and compromised for years. Facilities are painted and repaired, and custodial work is taken seriously. School appearance does not necessarily improve test scores, but it is an important symbol of how seriously the school authorities value educating the local population. The EMOs seem to have a major advantage in this area relative to the standard district administration.

12. Do EMOs Outperform Conventional Schools?

At this time there is little rigorous evidence comparing EMOs with comparable conventional schools. Some EMOs have reported superior results, but without the documentation required to substantiate the claims. Typically, they have reported that test scores have risen in most of their schools, but the specifics of which tests, how tests were administered, and which students were included is not given. Moreover, public schools have also raised tests in this new era of "standards" and high stakes testing and reporting in the public schools - in many cases, concentrating on test preparation rather than learning. So, the real issue is whether the test scores have risen in EMO schools at a faster rate than in comparable public schools when test scores are viewed as the currency of the realm.

Gary Miron and colleagues have done two studies that attempt to provide preliminary answers to this question. In their study of early Edison schools, they found about the same pattern in test scores between Edison schools and matched public schools (Miron & Applegate 2000). In their study of Michigan EMOs they found that the non-EMO, charter schools outscored those operated by EMOs (Miron & Nelson 2002: 143-145). Test scores are not the only indicators of success with respect to school reform, but there is even less evidence on other indicators.

13. Do EMOs Spur Competition?

Even if EMOs do not directly create breakthroughs in educational practices and results, they do offer an additional alternative to parents. Moreover, they may also spur competition with public schools and non-EMO charter schools by creating a more competitive environment. It is possible that they spur competition and improved results for the educational system, although there is no direct evidence on this matter. Hess (2002) has found that with more intense concentrations of charter schools and other alternatives, there is at least some emulation by the public schools of practices that may attract students. But, the overall results are fairly nominal, what Hess calls "revolution at the margins". In an analytic review of almost 40 econometric studies of competition, Belfield and Levin (2001) found modest effects (about a .1 standard deviation improvement in achievement for a one standard deviation increase in options). This improvement is comparable to about 10 points on the verbal Scholastic Aptitude Test (SAT), not a significant amount. Direct studies of the competitive effects of EMOs on student achievement or other outcomes are not available.

14. What Has Been Learned?

What has been learned in this first decade of for-profit EMOs? What we have learned is that contrary to the facile claims of their investment promoters, privatizing of operations of public schools is not a business that is easily convertible to profitability. Whatever the flaws of existing public school management and its poor performance in many urban areas, it does not appear that privatization, alone, is an effective answer. For-profit EMOs have generally not been profitable, nor is there evidence of breakthroughs in educational results. And, there is virtually no evidence that the quest for larger and larger numbers of schools will solve the dilemma through economies of scale.

This does not mean that for-profit EMOs or for-profit firms in elementary and secondary education will always fail to succeed. What it does mean is that the present model is unlikely to be the answer. In the spirit of experimentation, there are a number of directions that might be more promising:

- Smaller firms with a few schools are more consistent with the literature on economies of scale in education. Schools can be more easily managed and adapted to local conditions and can focus on improving effectiveness in a world of high variable costs. The single, for-profit school may hold promise for those committed to educational entrepreneurship. Close monitoring of costs and the needs of clientele are essential to make a profit in this challenging industry. It may also be possible for this type of endeavor to expand modestly with careful oversight.

- In the case of multiple schools, cost controls for central administration are important. The claims of some EMOs were that they could do a better job educationally at lower cost by avoiding the "waste" of central administration in public schools. The paradox is that their costs are considerably higher because of generous staffing, salaries, and benefits in their central headquarters – with stringent cost controls at school sites. Multiple-school companies will need to reverse this priority. Even so, it is not clear that a company can provide a unified brand of education over a large number of schools and school sites. Greater flexibility in school-site operations is required to adapt to different needs and contexts - while focusing the brand identification on goals and concepts rather than the uniformity of operations.

- Containing marketing and promotional costs is crucial. One strategy is to create outstanding demonstration schools, and to recruit new schools on the basis of demonstrated performance at existing ones. This strategy would call for a slower expansion, but one in which marketing costs could be reduced and a learning curve could be used more beneficially to improve operations.

- In the case of EMOs it is important to seek longer contracts, if possible, perhaps with performance benchmarks for each year on which payments will be based. The contract should be long enough to amortize fixed costs of starting-up at a site while providing reasonable assurance of completing the contract. In some cases the EMO might set its costs on the promise of a "turnkey" operation in which a dysfunctional school is returned to the district as a functional one - with certain performance criteria and incentives.

- Following successes in higher education, it is possible that the highest returns will be in niche markets. This has been the case in higher education where such firms as Apollo and its University of

Phoenix division have targeted older and fully employed workers providing conveniences such as parking and child care, modular courses of a standardized nature, practitioner teachers from the community at low cost, placement, and an ambitious approach to evaluation and quality control. DeVry has developed a profitable, niche market in providing preparation for technological careers. In both cases the niche consists of filling the needs of a specific clientele that is presently underserved, in a way that is attentive to costs and results. It is not an attempt to compete with conventional higher education. This fact alone reduces the political opposition that can be very costly to overcome by those attempting for-profit incursions into mainstream, public services.

- Niche markets can include special education where for-profit institutions have been successful historically. They can also include other groups of very high cost and at-risk students such as dropouts who are induced to return to school. But, in addition, they can include areas that are already profitable to some providers such as professional development, after-school services, counseling, administrative support (e.g. payroll, insurance, maintenance), and professional support services such as provision of curriculum, case studies, and software as some e-learning companies are doing. While these may sound less ambitious and less promising economically because they do not replace public schools, they can be highly profitable.

Two facts should give pause to those who believe that it will be easy to create a large for-profit network of EMO schools. The first is the dearth of for-profit schools that have entered the market historically among independent schools. This is probably less a matter of ignorance on the option of for-profit operation than of careful analysis. Elite private schools in the major metropolitan areas charge tuitions that are greater than $ 20,000 a year, two to three times what is spent for each pupil in the surrounding public schools. Yet, the for-profit sector has not been able to show a presence. Further, in addition to tuition, almost all independent schools engage in considerable fund-raising, with the highest tuition schools raising the most additional funding. (The same is found for private universities). Why haven't for-profit schools broken into this potential market in significant numbers to show what can be done with market incentives? This is worth contemplating by those who see large profits in operating or owning elementary and secondary schools.

Finally, this analysis is premised on existing methods of financing education. It is not clear how it might change if educational vouchers or tuition tax credits were to become widespread. My intuition tells me that a large enterprise with multiple schools would remain problematic. Certainly, this is the lesson to be learned from countries that have large for-profit sectors in elementary and secondary education such as Chile and the Asian countries with large numbers of for-profit schools.[9] To my knowledge, no corporate entity has become a major factor in private education in those countries.

---

9. For Chile see Carnoy & McEwan (2001).

References

Andrews, M. , Duncombe, W., & Yinger J. (2002) "Revisiting Economies of Size in American Education: Are We Any Closer to a Consensus?" *Economics of Education Review*, 21(3), pp. 245-62.

Belfield, C. & Levin, H. M. (2001) "The Effects of Competition on Educational Outcomes: A Review of the US Evidence", Occasional Paper 35, National Center for the Study of Privatization in Education, Teachers College, Columbia University, www.ncspe.org.

Brown, B. (1992) "Why Governments Run Schools," *Economics of Education Review*, 11(4), pp. 287-300.

Carnoy, M. & McEwan, P. (2001) "Privatization Through Vouchers in Developing Countries: The Cases of Chile and Colombia," In *Privatizing Education*, H. M. Levin, ed. (Boulder, CO: Westview).

Chubb, J. E. (2001) "The Profit Motive: The Private Can Be Public," *Education Matters* (Spring 2001), pp. 6, 8, 10, 12, 14.

Cookson, P. W., Jr. & Berger, K. (2002) *Expect Miracles: Charter Schools and the Politics of Hope and Despair* (Boulder, Co: Westview).

Cuban, L. (2001) *Oversold and Underused: Computers in the Classroom* (Cambridge, MA: Harvard University Press).

Driver, C. (2002) *Towards an Economic Model of School Principal Accountability*, Unpublished doctoral dissertation (Stanford, CA: School of Education, Stanford University).

Finn, C. E., Jr, Manno, B. V. & Vanourek, G. (2000) *Charter Schools in Action* (Princeton: Princeton University Press).

Hess, F. M. (2002) *Revolution at the Margins: The Impact of Competition on Urban School Systems* (Washington, D.C.: The Brookings Institution).

Levin, H. M. (1998) "Educational Vouchers: Effectiveness, Choice, and Costs," *Journal of Policy Analysis and Management*, 17(3), pp. 373-392.

Levin, H. M. (2001) "The Profit Motive: Bear Market," *Education Matters* (Spring 2001), pp. 6, 9, 11, 13, 15.

Merrill Lynch (1999) *The Book of Knowledge: Investing in the Growing Education and Training Industry*, In-depth Report (New York: Merrill Lynch & Co.).

Miron, G. & Applegate, B. (2000) *An Evaluation of Student Achievement in Edison Schools Opened in 1995 and 1996* (Kalamazoo, MI: The Evaluation Center, Western Michigan University).

Miron G. & Nelson, C. (2002) *What's Public About Charter Schools* (Thousand Oaks, CA: Corwin Press).

Murphy, J. & Shiffman, C. D. (2002) *Understanding and Assessing the Charter School Movement* (New York: Teachers College Press).

Richards, C. E., Shore, R. & Sawicky, M. B. (1996) *Risky Business: Private Management of Schools* (Washington, D.C.: Economic Policy Institute).

Tyack, D. (1974) *The One Best System* (Cambridge, MA: Harvard University Press).

Social Entrepreneurship edited by Marilyn L. Kourilsky and William B. Walstad
© *2003, Senate Hall Academic Publishing.*

7. Teacher-Ownership as Entrepreneurship in Public Education

Ted Kolderie

Center for Policy Studies, Minnesota

Abstract. Teacher ownership is a form of entrepreneurship with considerable potential to change the practices and performance of the K-12 institution. The idea is not now a part of the discussion: everywhere the 'given' has been that if you want to be a teacher you have to be an employee. Policy discussion assumes the employer/employee, boss/worker model. The discussion need not be confined in this way. The emergence of a teacher partnership in Minnesota, now running 11 schools, suggests it is entirely conceivable that the work in schools could be organized in ways that offer an ownership opportunity to the teachers. As owners, free to control their practice and accountable for learning, teachers might in their own interest make changes and improvements in the learning activity that it has proved impossible to secure from employees through management. At the moment the opportunities for all forms of entrepreneurship, and thus for entrepreneurship to improve learning, are constrained by the structure of the institution. The traditional arrangement - districts organized as bureaus; teachers employees – could hardly be more hostile; offering few if any openings through which entrepreneurs can be admitted. Entrepreneurship can have no effect on K-12 unless the institution is first opened – by 'policy entrepreneurship' – to arrangements other than the bureau model ... to contract arrangements of one kind or another. This can be done only by changing state law. It may prove easier to open the institution to professional teacher partnerships than to the widespread use of investor-owned commercial firms.

Keywords: teacher partnerships, teacher ownership, EdVisions.

1. Introduction

The all-too common assumption is not necessarily correct: that entrepreneurship will, perhaps must, take the form of an investor-owned, for-profit corporation. There are nonprofit organizations that display quite aggressive entrepreneurial behavior: People in both states may think quickly of Minnesota Public Radio, now expanding into southern California. And there are entrepreneurial agencies of government. A Minnesotan, again, might think of Minnesota Education Computing Consortium, which began early to make and sell instructional software to schools and which evolved in time into a private business organization.

This paper discusses yet another kind of organization, curiously unmentioned so far in the discussion about entrepreneurship in education. This is the partnership, or cooperative, as it might be used by teachers to carry on their professional work in public education.

2. The Policy Setting for Entrepreneurship and Innovation

'Entrepreneurship' cannot have any effect on education without a prior rearrangement of the institution that opens the way for entrepreneurs to appear. This will be clear from a real case involving a group of math teachers in Minnesota in the mid-1980s.

Bill Linder-Scholer, then the public-affairs officer for Cray Research, had made a small grant to a group of public-school math teachers in the Twin Cities metropolitan area to develop their plan for a small professional practice. The teachers were sure they knew what districts needed: a program to ensure that all 8th-grade students had a firm grasp of fundamentals before proceeding into 9th-grade algebra. In June, after the school year ended, they took their plan to a few superintendents. The superintendents agreed about the need. They said they would be interested on three conditions. First: That it would improve student learning. "We guarantee it", the teachers said. Second: That the cost would be reasonable. "We guarantee it," the teachers said. Third: That no one will get upset. The teachers closed their folders and left. Next year they were back in their regular classrooms. Everybody knew that of course someone would get upset.

2.1. The Absence of Incentives: No 'Reasons' and No Opportunities

There was no concept of contracting in the traditional district arrangement. Teachers were – are – employees. It would require a major effort to change so basic an arrangement; might involve a change in the master agreement between district and the union. That would be hard; would create tension; might cause a strike, even. Existing arrangements were comfortable for the adults in the organization. And no compelling need required the superintendent to take the risk of the math teachers' new program, to challenge the existing arrangement, even if the teachers' program would improve student learning. In Minnesota at that time the state did not require that students learned. The state was in the 'opportunity' business. It provided schools; required them to offer a minimum set of courses. Students were required to attend. They attended where they lived. Where they lived there was one organization offering public education, to whose schools they were assigned. Whether the students learned was up to them. You could tell the state did not care whether they learned, because it did not check ... did not test ... to see if they learned. The district organization got its revenue from the taxpayers, local and state, on the basis of student enrollment. Nothing important to the material success of the organization and the adults in it – not their revenues, not their salaries, not their pensions – in any significant way depended on whether the students learned. So the failure of students to learn provided no compelling reason to change arrangements in the district. The superintendent's primary concern about "whether someone would get upset" was therefore quite rational.

The institution was closed, generally, to entrepreneurs. It needed change. And there were new methods and technologies that might have brought improvement. There were entrepreneurs – individuals and organizations – who would like to have had a chance to show what they could do. And they did try. They sat patiently in the waiting room (figuratively), their 'black boxes' on their knees, waiting for the door to open so they could show the people inside all the good things the black box could do. But the door did not open. There were markets of private buyers available to them. John Golle and Frank Holmes were selling training to the securities industry before forming Education Alternatives, Inc.. But the prize was the public market. The Edison Project, when it appeared, did not spend a long time thinking about marketing private school to private families. Investors had also begun looking for vendors they could finance. Early in the '80s Jeff Lapides was going around the country looking for an opportunity to get in. The family had recently sold a business. He thought education had to be an opportunity: a third-of-a-trillion-dollar-a-year business; a business the customers were required by law to use; a business which did not have to charge its customers anything; a business in which there was universal third-party reimbursement, from tax sources, and in which you had an exclusive on the territory; in an industry full of badly-managed and technology-lagging organizations, in which payers and users and employees were all dissatisfied. He was told: There is no way in. It was hard to believe. How could there be all these needs and yet no opportunities, no market? But it was important to appreciate that distinction between a need and a market. It is not a good idea, in business, to mistake a need for a market. An industry cannot be sustained indefinitely by investors. There have to be buyers.

2.2. Chartering Has Provided an 'Opening'for Entrepreneurs

In the 1990s states began to enact laws that created a new sector within public education; that made it possible for some body other than the local district to start and operate a public school, and that in some cases made it possible for some body other than the local board to authorize such a school. With these laws the states were withdrawing the districts' traditional 'exclusive' to offer public education in the community. Even where they were sponsored by the local board these 'chartered' schools were outside the district framework; usually set up as non-profit corporation either under the state's existing law or under an equivalent provision of the chartering law. The schools could hire staff in the normal way. But they could also buy service; could contract for both 'instructional' and administrative services. In Michigan and Arizona, where the laws provided for non-district sponsors, the charters could be issued to commercial operators directly. The effect of this institutional innovation was to create a market for the services of entrepreneurs, a market in which the buyer was not a political body. As Michael Sandler noted in "The Emerging Education Industry" a paper reviewing its "first decade": "The charter movement provided an important stimulus to market growth by creating a more favorable environment in which schools could contract with private providers. Prior to charter school legislation most state law did not prohibit contracting, but school boards typically did not want to face the inevitable grievances from local teachers' unions which would entail costly litigation." (Sandler 2002), Quickly entrepreneurs began to move to the charter sector. Some initially did not; preferring to try for whole-district adoptions by boards of education rather than to get adoptions of their learning model school-by-school; preferring in effect to try to pick apples not by the apple but by the tree. Some of these, such as New American Schools, have now rethought this early decision.[1] Today about 10 per cent of the schools in the chartered sector are run by firms in 'the education industry'. Thomas Toch, writing a book about Edison Schools, says the company would not exist today had it not been for the chartering laws.[2] These now exist in almost every large state, enacted with strikingly bipartisan support and in virtually all cases against the opposition of the major associations in the K-12 institution.

This new sector of public education has begun to function as a "research and development" sector within K-12. The district sector is in the business of doing more or doing less, but not doing-different. The chartered sector contains incentives for schools to do-different. An incentive is a reason combined with an opportunity. It is not enough, if you want to cause things to happen, simply to give people a reason: Give people reasons but no opportunities and nothing results but frustration. Give people opportunities but no reasons to use them and nothing happens either. The chartered sector provides both. It provides an opportunity for schools to be created ... so, an opportunity for innovation ... and, because the schools are on an at-risk contract with their sponsor for fiscal and student performance, provides also a reason for them to be different. The laws give sponsors – even districts – incentives to seek out entrepreneurs, and give entrepreneurs incentives to seek out sponsors.

The chartered sector is, as Alan Odden has pointed out, this country's principal experiment with school-based decision-making.[3] Boards of

---

1. In its review of New American Schools RAND concluded: "Externally developed educational reform interventions cannot be 'break the mold' and still be marketable and implementable in current district and school contexts". *See Facing the Challenges of Whole-school Reform: New American Schools after a Decade.* RAND, 2000.
2. Conversation with the author, 2000.
3. See *Financing Schools for High Performance: Strategies for Improving the Use of Educational Resources*, Allan Odden and Carolyn Busch, Jossey-Bass, 1998.

education are often urged to delegate authority to the school, and boards often affirm they do delegate, but in the district sector this is usually more rhetoric than reality. For the chartered school, by contrast, on contract to its sponsor, there is a real delegation of meaningful authority. The school is responsible for its budget, for assembling its teachers, for managing its own facilities and support services and, most important, for selecting its learning program. This combination of accountability and autonomy means it has a need for, and can be a real market for, quality services. Some of the schools staff up, rather than 'buy'. Some that buy a learning design select a known and traditional programs of learning; do not want to be innovative. But some are in the market for innovative programs, and buy such programs when these are offered. Sylvan Learning (to take one example) is a vendor of learning services – as, to Appleton WI where Thomas Scullen, the superintendent, set up a charter 'virtual' school to enroll homeschoolers using the Calvert Home Study curriculum provided by Sylvan. Arizona Benefit Systems is a vendor just of 'back office' services; leaves the learning program to those who run the school.

It is at the moment hard to see all this: Most of what passes for research on the chartered schools asks questions that are simply descriptive: about the location of the school, its size, the number and nature of its students and teachers, etc. ... or tries to evaluate student performance "in chartered schools" – a kind of evaluation that has little real meaning; that is essentially a part of the political debate. A chartered school is not a kind of school, not a learning program or pedagogy. It is an empty institutional structure, as a building is an empty physical structure. No student learns anything from an empty structure. In both cases, what students learn depends on what is put into that structure: the learning program, the people, the 'culture'. There has been too little good work done to describe what the schools in this new sector are as schools, and to identify which of these characteristics then make a difference to student motivation and student performance.

3. The Appearance of the Teacher Professional Partnership

In 1994, sponsored by their local district, a group of teachers and others set up an unusual chartered school in a small city in south-central Minnesota: a 7-12 secondary, essentially ungraded, with no courses and no classes and, most interestingly, no employees. The board of the nonprofit that is legally the Minnesota New Country School has – manages – only contracts. There is a contract with the district for some transportation and extracurriculars, one with a caterer for lunch, another with a building-owner for space. The school's largest contract – for the learning program and the operation of it – is with EdVisions. This is an organization formed by the teachers. Legally it is a Chapter 308A under Minnesota law; a (workers') cooperative. Generically it is a small professional partnership. Through the partnership the teachers select their colleagues, decide the methods and materials, make the work-assignments, evaluate performance and decide their own compensation.

3.1. The School with No Courses, No Classes and No Employees

For several years the Minnesota New Country School operated out of storefronts on Main Street in LeSueur. In 1998 it moved into a new building built for it by a community development group in Henderson, six miles north/ downriver. The partnership also began to grow. It took on three elementary schools. And it began to open new secondary schools. Some are in southern Minnesota; one is in Duluth; several are in the Twin Cities metropolitan area. When school opened in fall 2002 EdVisions had 11 schools. The schools vary but in some virtually all the work is project-based. Students, with their teacher-advisers and their parents, shape their interests into projects structured to connect them with the areas of knowledge set out in the state graduation requirements. Some are individual projects; some are group projects. There is a computer work station for every student: The large open room looks like a newspaper city room or, as one consultant said, "like a messy Kinko's". The computers, on the internet all day long, are the students' access to the world of information available on the web.

Within the partnership the tradeoffs between adult interests and student interests appear to be made with integrity. If the cooperative underpays its member-teachers it will not have teachers; so will not have schools. If it shorts its students it will not have students; so will not have schools. The practice is to include students in decisions about who comes in to teach. "The kids are going to decide in 15 minutes whether to eat you alive or to let you live," says Dee Thomas, the lead teacher at New Country. "We need to have people the students will work with."[4] Students choose their advisers. Over time an adviser not-chosen may be asked to leave, and some teachers have been dropped. As with students, this model is not for everyone. Patterns of expenditure are quite different from those in district schools. Staffing requirements are lower, so individual advisers make more than they would as instructors in district schools in this part of the state. During the salary review some teachers get raises; some may not. The model is still evolving: It has been a learning process. Until 2002, as additional schools were created, the partnership – the cooperative, EdVisions – simply expanded. This made the EdVisions responsible for decisions actually made site-by-site. So EdVisions has tried to create smaller partnerships for these school-level decisions, with EdVisions becoming a service organization for the school sites; a 'co-op of co-ops'.

---

4.   The remark occurs often in her presentation to visitors to New Country School.

The New Country/EdVisions model is closely watched. [Both have websites: <www.mncs.k12.mn.us> and <www.edvisions.coop>.] The Henderson school gets a lot of visitors, from around the country and from other countries. One visitor, in April 2000, was Tom Vander Ark, head of the education program for the Bill & Melinda Gates Foundation. The foundation quickly made an investment of $4.5 million in the replication of this model and another, later, to take the model national.

No one can tell yet whether, as owners, other teachers in other partnerships would also set up their school/program on the project-based model.[5] There is no reason why they would need to: Ownership could be combined with other learning models. On the other hand, there are clear reasons why they might. Students like the way project-based learning individualizes and personalizes their work. More-motivated students work more seriously. As the students take more responsibility for their own learning the staffing requirements change, as the teacher's role changes from specialist to generalist. So therefore do the school's expenditures. This shift in expenditures itself has major implications. The New Country model shows that it is possible to have a small high school (120 students in the six grades 7-12) that is both educationally and economically viable. This 'discovery' – from this innovative school in which the learning program is designed and owned by teachers – is enormously important everywhere for small communities with declining enrollments; told at the moment that their only choices are to raise taxes to maintain the course-and-class model or to close and consolidate.

4. The Idea of Teacher Ownership is Generalizable

The ownership model – in use, of course, in most professional fields – is probably usable and workable in education as well. Like lawyers, doctors, accountants, architects, consultants, and others, teachers could have – and probably should have – an option to work for themselves, alone or as partners with others in single- or multi-specialty groups. The traditional arrangement in K-12, in which teachers work as employees for administrators, is not essential ... almost certainly is only historic. The original model has simply persisted, unchanged.

The ownership idea had briefly appeared in policy discussion in Minnesota in the 1980s; then was laid aside. It revived about 2000 as EdVisions' success became apparent. A project headed by Edward J. Dirkswager undertook to

---

5. In the case of New Country School the decision to form the school came first. The idea of ownership appeared later. Arguably, however, the teachers felt like owners from the beginning since Minnesota law provided for a school to be proposed by teachers and for teachers to form a majority of the board of the school.

think through the what, the why and the how of teacher-ownership, working with a task force of persons from education, from the cooperative movement and from the professions organized on a partnership basis. Its book, *Teachers As Owners*, was published by Scarecrow Press in June 2002.[6]

There is no 'right' model; no 'one best way'. Clearly 'ownership' could take a different form than it has in New Country/EdVisions. It is important for everyone in the discussion to understand that at almost every point there are multiple options.

- Teachers' professional organizations could use any of the several forms of organization provided by the laws of the states: partnerships, cooperatives (as with EdVisions), limited-liability companies, etc. A special statute could be created just for teacher partnerships.

- EdVisions operates whole, discrete schools. A partnership could also work at a scale either larger or smaller than a whole school. Teachers might form a partnership to run a department of a school: A partnership might provide, say, the science department of a big suburban high school. Or a partnership might form to operate a program serving multiple schools districtwide, or multiple districts. In Minneapolis, for example, the teachers at the elementary Montessori sites might form a partnership and contract with the board of education for the work they now do as employees.

- EdVisions' teachers handle both the learning program and the administrative responsibilities for their schools. It would be possible, equally, for the teachers in the partnership to handle only the learning program of the school, leaving the board of the school to hire administrators to run the 'support services'. Or the partnership might contract to handle both the learning program and the administration but – in the manner of many law firms and physician clinics – employ itself the administrative and clerical personnel.

- Partnerships could serve a variety of 'clients'. EdVisions serves mainly secondary students in the charter sector of K-12. A partnership could contract directly with a district, to serve either an elementary or a secondary school. With its tax credit in 1997 Minnesota created a public but user-directed market for educational

---

6.   See *Teachers As Owners: A Key to Revitalizing Public Education*, edited by Edward J. Dirkswager, Scarecrow Press, 2002.

services. The tax credit cannot be used for schoolwork leading to a diploma but can be used for supplementary work: summer school, language programs, tutoring, etc. This market could be served by teacher partnerships. Partnerships could also serve the markets for learning outside the K-12 years. They might help educate adults; perhaps employees in the corporate training market. They could train teachers, especially in the methods of project-based learning. There is really no limit on the types of clients that could be served.

In June 2003 Public Agenda, an opinion-survey organization based in New York, publishzed its finding about what teachers think of their jobe, their life, and their unions. The survey contained one question touching on ownership: "How interested wuld you be in working at a charter school that was run and manged by teachers themselves?"

The question hardly conveys the essence of the partnership idea, and asked teachers to affirm a willingness to move into the chartered sector as a condition of having the opportunity to 'run the school'. Still, the results were quite stunning:

Fifty-eight per cent of all teachers would be somewhat or very interested in having that arrangement (36 per cent not-interested). Sixty-five per cent of those with less than five years experience were interested (25 per cent not). And fifty per cent of 'verterans', with more than 20 years experience, said they would be interested.[7]

5.   Ownership Has Significant Implications for the 'Improvement' Agenda

This non-traditional arrangement, with its very different set of incentives for teachers, represents a 'driver' for change and is therefore potentially a major strategy for policy. Policy ought not to be about designing end-state 'ideal' schools. Policy ought to be about finding ways to cause the people in K-12 to change and improve ... about giving educators and others reasons and opportunities to design new and better schools/schooling themselves: on their own initiative, in their own interest and from their own resources. For policy leadership the idea, strategically, is always to look for "the one thing that leads on to everything else" ... to "Start with the change that creates the most pressure for other constructive changes", as Richard Murnane and Frank Levy put it. (Murnane and Levy 2000) Teacher ownership in a charter context is such a "place to start".

7.   *Stand by Me: What Teachers Really Think about Unions, Merit Pay and Other Professional Matters.* Public Agenda, New York, June 2003.

The effort to improve public education is stuck at the moment on a number of points having to do with teachers and teaching. Some useful progress might begin if the assumption of employment were pulled out and the questions were then re-thought on the assumption that teachers were, instead, owners.

How to get teachers into professional roles – Albert Shanker's effort in the late 1980s following the *Nation at Risk* report – to make the improvement of education the improvement of teaching and of the professional status of teachers – did not succeed. Teachers continued as essentially civil servants employed by and directed by administrators. In some respects collective bargaining may have helped lock teachers into this civil-service-employee status: The unions have won their members most everything on their economic agenda but boards of education have been able to protect the area of 'professional issues' as 'management rights'. Boards are not about to turn over the control of the learning activity to teachers with no visible accountability for performance; and within the traditional framework of employment the unions' only answer – "Trust us" – has not been good enough.[8]

The dynamics of this discussion change dramatically when teachers as a group accept a performance contract to organize and run a learning program. Within the framework of such an agreement the teacher-group gets full control of the professional issues ... of how the job is to be done. The teachers control the admission to their group; sets the standards of practice; select the methods and materials; make the work assignments; run the program for the improvement of professional practice; assess the quality of practice and decide the rewards for practice within their group ... decide their own compensation. This is virtually everything the unions have been trying to get for their members through legislation or through bargaining and without notable success. It may be possible to get teachers to professional status faster through ownership than through bargaining.

How to change teacher practice and improve student learning – Teachers in a partnership are given a lump of money, given full authority to arrange the learning program, required to show that the students learn, and allowed to keep for use in their program or as personal income what they do not need to spend. [This is in the 'pure' partnership. For a variation see the discussion about Milwaukee, below.] This gives them an incentive – a reason combined with an opportunity – to look for different and better ways to arrange schooling; gives them an incentive to be entrepreneurial. Once in this position they may move quickly to introduce practices that reduce costs and improve student learning. If a long conversation with math teachers one evening in the mid-'80s is any guide, they would get students working independently as fast as they could go. They would get kids helping other kids. They would use community resources.

8.   See *Teaching the New Basic Skills*, Richard J. Murnane and Frank Levy, The Free Press, 1996, page 224.

They would get parents involved, at the home end. They would differentiate the staffing; sharing duties. And they would greatly expand the use of new learning technology.[9] Most important, perhaps, teachers might shift to project-based learning. They would make the students responsible for their own learning. They would begin with what students want to know; connecting the projects then to state standards about what students need to know. In EdVisions' experience students respond positively to this: They work hard, they are interested, and discipline problems virtually disappear. EdVisions' schools do not teach to the test, but "passing the test" turns out not to be a problem.

How to enlarge the supply of quality teachers – K-12 is having a major problem in holding teachers, and to some degree in attracting top-quality teachers. Most of the solutions proposed for this problem look toward recruitment, education and 'professional development'. As with the shortage of administrators the idea is to get better people for the job. But such an effort is unlikely to succeed without an effort also to create a better job for the people; to make teaching a more successful and therefore more rewarding occupation. Teachers may be much more attracted to a model in which students are interested and problems of discipline and control are reduced. Professional groups of teachers could run math and/or science programs in large high schools, on contract either to the district or (if site-managed) to a school; perhaps in time serving several schools and/or districts. Applied at the department level the 'partnership' model may be especially helpful in relieving the shortage of teachers in key specialty areas.

How to speed the introduction of learning technology – Within existing arrangements it is hard to get new information technology into the schools; hard to get it used to its potential; hard to keep it up to date. Teachers' unions work in negotiations primarily to increase salaries, which reduces the money available for the usually add-on costs of computers, software and internet connections. Where the computer hardware and software is introduced the teachers are often uncomfortable with it; uncomfortable feeling they know less about it than do the students. Teachers may also see it as reducing their (traditional) function in 'instruction'; in plain words, costing jobs. Putting computers in schools with conventional teacher-instruction is, Lewis Perelman says, "like putting afterburners on horses: They are not compatible technologies".[10]

When the teachers are owners the different incentives may produce a different result. Teachers will then have a strong incentive – again, a reason

---

9. Author's conversation with teachers in the Rosemount-Apple Valley district in Minnesota, 1986.
10. See *School's Out: Hyperlearning, the New Technology and the End of Education*, Lewis J. Perelman, William Morrow and Company, Inc. 1992. Chapter 1 begins with the transition to the automobile from the "horseless carriage".

and an opportunity – to make the changes in their practice that computers and the web imply, and will be in a position to benefit directly from whatever the new technology can do both to improve student learning (on which their own success now will depend) and to reduce the cost of school-operation. Where work and ownership are combined new technology gets taken up rapidly: Think about American agriculture after 1870. Farmers quickly picked up the new machinery, the new seeds, the new cropping-practices. Incomes rose and prices declined. If teachers were owners they might behave like farmers.

How to contain costs and maintain program – In the district sector we assume the process of bargaining between the board of education and the union will work effectively to balance appropriately the competing demands for program and class-size, on the one hand, and for teacher-compensation on the other. Unhappily this bargaining process for the 'balancing of interests' does not work as well in practice as it does in theory. In the negotiations the union pushes to get more for its members. The board and superintendent, who in theory represent the public and student interest, in fact simply resist, trying mainly to avoid a strike. Knowing they cannot win a strike they know it is pointless to resist demands that may cause a strike. In this unequal contest students lose. The districts end up overspending the legislative allocation of new revenue; then ... complaining that the Legislature "has not given us enough" ... cut program and raise class size and as quickly as possible return to the voters or to the Legislature for money to "restore the cuts". To the extent revenue-increases lag behind, program – and staff – must be reduced. This hurts the whole enterprise, including the teachers who are laid off.

Where teachers are owners – in a school, in a department or in a district-wide program – the trade-off between compensation and program ... between adult interests and student interests ... is internalized within a single group. The history in EdVisions is that the tradeoff is made with integrity.[11]

5.1. A Variation That Lets Teachers Remain in District Employment Has Potential in the Cities

When introduced into Wisconsin it became clear quickly that the ownership idea did not fit. Under Wisconsin law schools are chartered mainly by districts,

---

11. At the 1999 annual meeting of New Country School and its sponsoring district two members of the district board asked Brian Swenson, chair of the board of the school, how it was possible to contain costs and to end the year in the black.. The district at that point still had not settled its contract with the union. "I don't have anything to do with it," Swenson said. "The teachers are not our employees". Members of EdVisions tried to explain. Finally one said: "We had to ask ourselves how we could tell the kids they were not going to get an upgrade in their software next year because we wanted to take out more in salary for ourselves".

the schools are 'instrumentalities' of the district and teachers, if they wish to remain in the state retirement program (as most do) must remain employees of the district. This became an issue for a group of teachers in Milwaukee who wanted to start an elementary school and who wanted to form as a cooperative. One of the teachers took this to her father, who had for 25 years worked as an official for the American Federation of State County and Municipal Employees. He talked about it with a friend who had worked in labor law. Their solution was to split the teachers' life, keeping 'the economic side' with district employment, the master contract and union membership and forming the cooperative as a vehicle just for the teachers' professional life.

This worked. The I.D.E.A.L. charter school completed its first year in June 2002 with 198 students in four rooms at the end of the second floor of a Milwaukee middle school. Milwaukee makes a big delegation of program autonomy to its chartered schools. The teachers collectively hold the charter. The teachers continue as district employees. They are paid the contract rate for teachers but they can decide how many teachers of what type to have; so can reallocate expenditures. There is a memorandum of understanding with the Milwaukee Teachers Education Association, the bargaining agent for the district's teachers, waiving certain provisions of the master contract. The union cooperates: These teachers are, after all, its members. And the board of education is happy. The teachers are protected, and end up with full control of 'professional issues'.

6. Those Interested in Entrepreneurship Might Usefully Encourage Teacher Ownership

As presently organized the commercial education industry is having a hard time getting established in K-12 public education. Most of its members today are "for-profit" firms. And the resistance to "for-profits" is intense. The charter sector has provided a market; the nonprofit school serving as a kind of 'cartilege' separating the political sponsor from the for-profit vendor. But even in this sector the opposition is tough. And where the firms are trying to secure contracts directly with districts the going is tougher still; painful, like trying to connect bone-to-bone directly. In truth, the 'education industry' is more successful outside K-12; especially in higher education and in private markets such as corporate training. It is attracted to K-12 because of its size. But its strategy is traditional; unimaginative. It accepts the single-district model of organization, and the 'technology' of teachers-talking; students-listening-and-reciting. It tries – as Sandler's paper for the Education Industry Leadership Board makes clear – to sell materials and services that 'supplement' this traditional classroom: testing programs, textbook-equivalents, reference materials, professional development and various aids both for students and for teachers. (Sandler 2002)

Efforts continue, nevertheless, to win contracts with districts to operate schools. A recent effort has been to get the state to intervene in big-city situations ... not to run the district or to give it to the mayor to run, but to install a new state-created board and new managers that will contract the running of schools to others – including commercial firms. This has been tough going, too, as recent developments in Pennsylvania make clear. Teacher unions are reported investing about $50 million in the effort to block contracting, on the argument that 'for-profit' is bad for the public; an argument the media usually pass on at face value.

Aware of the skepticism it faces with the public as well as the hostility it faces with the unions, the industry seems to be pinning its hopes now on the new electronics: If the public can be persuaded to like this new technology and if the industry can get itself associated in the public mind with the technology then perhaps the public can be persuaded to like the industry.

Taking existing arrangements as given, the industry is marketing the technology to district administrators, confident that if they would just take the time to understand the 'black box' they would surely want to buy it. This is problematic. As presently organized K-12 is not very interested in introducing productive new technologies if to do so would create stress in its schools and among its teachers. Districts sometimes buy the technology (or accept it when it is given) but do not require that the teachers use it. Teachers do not always want to use it; or know how to use it. Like other workers when new machinery is introduced, they may resist; 'go Luddite'.

As we saw above, the new technology might be taken up much faster if the decision were in the hands of teachers acting in their own interest. It is revealing to ask – say, those math teachers – what they would do if they were a group, were free to redesign and run their own program, were required to demonstrate student learning, but were given the per-pupil amount and were free to keep for use in the program or as personal income what they did not need to spend.[12] They might ask themselves: What could we do that would improve student learning that would not require us to spend money we could otherwise keep? 'Technology' would be part of their answer. This is quite unlike the proposition with which teachers are faced when told by the superintendent: Here's a new machine. Learn it and use it. No, you will not be paid more.

Not surprisingly, that effort to this point has not been very successful. The newsletters covering "the education industry" are filled mainly with stories about companies getting venture capital and buying each other up; not with stories about companies getting contracts. The companies might better be

---

12. Cf page 12.

marketing to teacher-groups, which would have an incentive to pick up technologies that could make their work easier, more successful and more rewarding. Strategically, therefore, those interested in expanding entrepreneurship and increasing its impact on education should be working now to rearrange K-12 so it is teachers rather than administrators who have the opportunity and the reasons to make the decisions about the acquisition of learning technology. At the moment those in the industry and/or interested in entrepreneurship do not see this. "I haven't got time to talk to the teachers," an executive of Control Data said when this was suggested to him in the '80s.[13] They need to be helped to see this.

6.1. The Teacher-Partnership Vs. the Corporation

The difficulties and limitations of entrepreneurship in the corporate, for-profit model have been well described in another paper for this symposium (Levin 2002). To date, argues Henry Levin, the 'education management organization' has not become profitable; has not been able to generate economies of scale as the various companies attempt to establish a national 'brand' of school. In addition, the political and ideological opposition has been intense, slowing growth and adding further to cost. Levin also says the EMOs have produced neither innovative school designs nor exemplary educational results.

The contrast with the EdVisions cooperative is merely suggestive. This is one partnership, running 11 schools. Still: Its growth rate has been impressive. Its economics are sound. (New Country School has received letters from the state saying its balances are getting too high.) Its project-based learning represents a radical shift away from traditional 'methods'. Its use of internet technology is exemplary. The break with the traditional 'employment' arrangement ... the shift to a contract with a teacher-cooperative ... creates an entirely new form of governance. All these together would seem to qualify the EdVisions model as innovative: as exactly the rapid and radical change in traditional arrangements that advocates hope would result from an entrepreneurial effort to change school and schooling.

The effect of an innovative school on the educational system more generally is a different question. New schools do not change existing schools. Existing schools are changed by the districts that own and run them. And the districts are extremely resistant: not very interested in change and not really able to make more than incremental changes in their methods and their practices. This resistance is a problem the states will need to deal with directly,

---

13. Author's conversation with William Ridley, at the time also a member of the Minnesota State Board of Education.

at some point. It is unlikely to be overcome by the introduction of exemplary models of school.

7. Implications for Teaching and Research about Entrepreneurship

An academic institution that broadened its concept of entrepreneurship enough to include the professional partnership might usefully broaden its teaching about partnerships beyond the field of education. Nurses, some years ago, moved to professional status; able to take primary responsibility for certain types of patient care. It might be useful in designing a course to look at the academic preparation of what are now called 'nurse-practitioners' and at the kind of education these professionals receive.[14] It might be useful to study the way nurse-practitioners organize and work, in (solo and group) practice. It might be useful to examine, similarly, groups of professionals in law, consulting, engineering and architecture. In Philadelphia workers' cooperatives have been formed to run child day care centers.[15] It is possible that in the early years – when there are so few partnerships of teachers in practice – the experience from these other fields will be essential for a successful effort to train teachers for this new and different pattern of practice. There will be some interesting question to think through: whether, for example, this teaching about partnerships occurs in the school of education or in the school of business, or in some joint program between the two.

There are significant implications also for the schools of public policy and management. Gradually, in major universities, these have been coming into the area earlier reserved to the departments of education policy and administration in the schools of education. Entrepreneurship and radically changed arrangements for teachers now raise questions the schools of public affairs will want to take up themselves; including questions about how to generate the changes in the policy framework needed for entrepreneurship in the school sector.

There will also be a need to educate public bodies to 'buy right'. The interest in entrepreneurship has probably focused on the entrepreneurs; on the (prospective) vendors. But there must also be willing and capable buyers if entrepreneurs are to find a market. Far too little attention has been given to the buyer side. It is hard to find a school of public management – or, for that matter, a school of business management – that teaches how to buy-smart;

---

14. In her course for nurse-practitioners at the College of St. Catherine in Saint Paul MN Dodie Russell has used a text titled *The Nurse Entrepreneur*. See "Nurse Practitioners and Teacher Practitioners", Public Services Redesign Project, July 1984, available from the author.
15. See "ChildSpace: A Nonprofit + Workers' Cooperative", Public Services Redesign Project, July 1993.

teaches the theory, the strategy and the practices of contracting. This is a serious gap in the academic program for entrepreneurship, that needs to be filled quickly.

7.1. Opportunities for Research and Consulting

Research will be essential for any successful teaching about partnerships, since – again – so many of the cases in the early years will have to be found outside education. In addition to the experience in what Thomas DeLong at Harvard Business School calls "professional service organizations" it might be useful to look at the 'leased department' as this practice has appeared in large retail organizations. This would provide a look at the buyer side: at the decisions by owners of retail stores not to own but to bring into the store, on lease, selected departments owned and run by others.[16] It would be interesting also to look at teachers who now run, and successfully, businesses on the side: during the school year or during the summer.[17] The research and the teaching together will also provide a basis for outreach, service and consulting – showing others how to set up and run partnerships in education, and showing districts and their boards how to buy. The consulting, of course, further enriches the research and teaching.

8. Conclusion

Entrepreneurship' is not synonymous with 'the education industry'; with investor-owned, 'for-profit' and corporate. If 'entrepreneurship' means starting-things, trying things, doing-different we do need to recognize that other kinds of organizations can do this too. Nonprofits can; some 'bureaus' do. It depends on having the system-incentives properly designed and structured to encourage this behavior. Now we see examples of significant entrepreneurship and innovation emerging in professional partnerships owned by teachers, under new arrangements that give teachers an opportunity to benefit from the productivity-gains that result from improvements they introduce. This is a conceivable arrangement. It is worth serious consideration by teachers. And surely also by boards of education and state policy leadership,

---

16. See "Owned vs. Leased Departments and Some Implications for Schools", Public Services Redesign Project, April 1988.
17. Bob Rose owned and ran a college-scarf business while president of the Minneapolis Federation of Teachers; Robert Astrup owned and ran a group of Nautilus Clubs before becoming president of the Minnesota Education Association. "Take a look at teacher ownership of summer camps", Myron Lieberman suggests. (Letter to the author.)

which lack a strategy for introducing change and improvement and have no real idea how they can change teacher practice.

Presentations on the idea were scheduled for Novembers 2003 in Washington D.C. for the annual meeting of the National Board of Professional Teaching Standards, with Teach For America and with the U.S. Department of Education. It was also discussed with Teachers Union Reform Network in Seattle in February 2003.

At the moment there is mainly the idea. But it is always good not to speak disrespectfully of small beginnings.

References

Dirkswager, Edward J., editor   (2002) *Teachers As Owners: A Key to Revitalizing Public Education*, Lanham MD: Scarecrow Press.

Kolderie, Ted "The Two Different Concepts of Privatization" (1986) *Public Administration Review* 46(4) page 285.

Murnane, Richard J. and Levy, Frank (1996) *Teaching the New Basic Skills,* New York: The Free Press, page 224.

Odden, Allan and Busch, Carolyn (1998) *Financing Schools for High Performance: Strategies for Improving the Use of Educational Resources,* San Francisco: Jossey-Bass.

Perelman, Lewis J. (1992) *School's Out: Hyperlearning, the New Technology and the End of Education*, New York: William Morrow and Company, Inc.

8. Educational Entrepreneurship and Covisionary Multisectorism

Marilyn L. Kourilsky
UCLA

Guilbert Hentschke
USC

Abstract. This paper introduces the concept of "educational multisectorism" among the private not-for-profit, private for profit, and public/government sectors. Multisectorism leverages the opportunities presented by the contrasting economic and "social" advantages (and disadvantages) of educational organizations operating in the three sectors, as viewed through the analytical prism of comparative advantage. The underlying principle of multisectorism is the belief that drawing on the resources and strengths of all three sectors can be of significant benefit to the pursuit of educational reform. Thus, multisectorism (rather than "unisectorism") – and the covisionary entrepreneurial thinking and social entrepreneurship that are its implementation alter egos is suggested as a powerful paradigm for innovation and change. Through this paradigm, educators, regardless of sector location, can join forces to advance K-12 educational and social outcomes. The authors emphasize the tight coupling between educational entrepreneurship and social entrepreneurship and the evolutionary changes that are beginning to foster both processes in K-12 education. They also examine the education "industry" today – its historical antecedents and the current trends that are shaping it – and delve into the "industry's" expanded three-sector modern presence that extends well beyond traditional schools, colleges, and universities. Robust and client serving educational ventures that maximize educational reform and learning improvement may best grow from the cross-sectoral synergy of sector-specific advantages. The fashioning and sustaining of such effective "covisionary educational multisectorism" will hinge on educational leadership that pursues its social mission across sector lines and that is firmly grounded in the characteristics and principles (as defined in this paper) of educational entrepreneurship and entrepreneurial thinking.

Keywords: K-12 education, educational reform, educational entrepreneurship, social entrepreneurship, entrepreneurial thinking, comparative advantage, public and private sectors, cross-sector educational initiatives, educational leadership.

1. Introduction and Overview

The emerging connections between the world of education and the world of entrepreneurship are a natural part of the spirited debate about the "how," the "by whom," and the "for whom" of K-12 education. The attitudes, thought processes, and skills of entrepreneurial thinking and social entrepreneurship have the capacity to link successfully with the social objectives of K-12 education in <u>all three of the major sectors of economic activity</u>: private not-for-profit, private for profit, and public/government. By contrasting the intrinsic economic and "social" advantages (and implicit disadvantages) of educational organizations in these sectors as viewed through the prism of comparative advantage, one can begin to explore their natural "specializations" with respect to educational entrepreneurship.[1] In this paper, the authors introduce the notion of "educational multisectorism" – the belief that drawing on the resources and strengths of all three sectors can be of significant benefit to the pursuit of educational reform.[2] A theme running through this paper is that "educational multisectorism" (rather than "unisectorism") – and the covisionary social entrepreneurship which is its implementation alter ego – represent a powerful paradigm for innovation and change around which educators, regardless of sector location, can join forces to advance K-12 educational and social outcomes.

We begin by defining educational entrepreneurship and discussing how manifestations of educational entrepreneurship may vary with the levels of the entrepreneurial spectrum pyramid. The next section seeks to describe evolutionary changes that we believe are beginning to foster the growth of educational entrepreneurship in K-12 education. The subsequent sections shift the spotlight to the education "industry" today, its historical antecedents, the current trends that are shaping it, and its expanded modern presence well beyond traditional schools, colleges, and universities. As the discussion evolves, we seek to extend our prior analyses to argue that K-12 education is rapidly evolving into a three-sector (as opposed to primarily governmental) domain; and that each sector enjoys certain respective comparative advantages relative to various types of educational objectives, organizations and ventures. Attention is called to a collateral risk of this surge of educational innovation – "deprofessionalizing" teaching – and the need to ensure that the complexities of educational decision-making are still guided and informed by the expertise and experience of the professional educator. We further develop the idea that robust and client serving educational ventures that maximize educational reform and learning improvement may best grow from the cross-sectoral synergy of these (sector-specific) advantages. Further, the fashioning and sustaining of effective, covisionary "educational multisectorism" will hinge on educational leadership that is firmly grounded in the characteristics and principles (as defined in this paper) of educational entrepreneurship and entrepreneurial thinking.

---

1.   Unfortunately, there is a growing tendency within public and academic discourse to allow the concept of educational entrepreneurship to be held "hostage" under the controversial umbrella of educational privatization – with all of its (often polarizing) connotations of purely private for profit ownership and that ownership's potential challenge to the public sector's role in the provision of education.
2.   Multisectorism is a new term also introduced by the authors.

2. Educational Entrepreneurship

There are many definitions of entrepreneurship that have been suggested in the literature. However, a close examination reveals a fairly small number of core elements that they share. These include recognizing and acting on opportunities, marshalling resources and adding value, taking risks, articulating a compelling vision, initiating ventures, and modifying strategic and tactical plans on a regular basis to adapt to changing circumstances. Or, even more succinctly, entrepreneurs are "innovative, opportunity-oriented, resourceful, value-creating change agents," (Dees, Emerson & Economy, 2001).

Key to the implementation of these components is a combination of mindset and attitudes that can be called entrepreneurial thinking. In that spirit, Kourilsky (1995) frames the concept of entrepreneurship as an orientation or means of observing the world – "...the ability to *recognize* an opportunity that others have overlooked and the insight, self-esteem, and courage to *act* where others have hesitated."

From these definitions, one can see immediately that entrepreneurship and entrepreneurial thinking are not just about creating enterprises – but about bringing to bear on problems and opportunities in the public, not-for-profit, and for profit sectors a rich framework of skills, intellectual attributes, and innovative approaches. The concept of social entrepreneurship adds a further layer to the picture – entrepreneurship practice and entrepreneurial thinking in the pursuit of a social mission.

In this paper, we choose to have the term educational entrepreneurship always carry with it the implicit connotation of social entrepreneurship. In other words, for the purposes of our discussion, just creating a viable enterprise in the educational marketplace is not sufficient to qualify as educational entrepreneurship. We reserve the phrase educational entrepreneurship to be about applying the skills and attitudes inherent in entrepreneurial thinking and the entrepreneurial process to achieve innovative and sustainable impact and reforms with respect to the social mission of K-12 education, regardless of the ownership profile of the institution or venture under discussion.

The entepreneurial spectrum pyramid (Figure 1 below) developed by Kourilsky (1995) is a helpful lens through which to view the manifestations of educational entrepreneurship in the not-for-profit, for profit, and public sectors.

Figure 1: Entrepreneurial Spectrum Pyramid

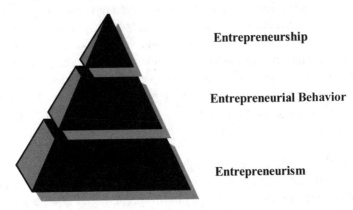

Entrepreneurship

Entrepreneurial Behavior

Entrepreneurism

"Entrepreneurship." The top level of the pyramid carries the label of the noun "entrepreneurship." Educational venture initiators (or the venture initiation team) occupy this first level of the pyramid. It is their foresight and efforts that first transform the vapor of an idea into tangible value. Initiators innovate and create by recognizing educational opportunities that can advance the social mission of education, conjuring ideas and a long-run vision of what they would like to accomplish, and implementing a plan to bring their ideas and vision to reality. Initiators typically bear the greatest share of the risk burden associated with the undertaking of an entrepreneurial pursuit.

It is primarily the raw passion, horsepower, and determination of the founding team that carries educational ventures successfully through their initial conception and start-up phases. However, if a venture wants to embark on serious growth beyond these early stages, it eventually must broaden its leadership base to tap into the resources of an entrepreneurial development team.

"Entrepreneurial Behavior." The members of the entrepreneurial development team occupy the middle level of the pyramid, the Entrepreneurial Behavior level. This level focuses on the adjective *entrepreneurial* rather than on the noun *entrepreneurship*. As such, the members of this level are not themselves the initiators – the catalytic agents with the innovative impulse to jumpstart the venture from zero. However, they are expert practitioners in their own right of much of the thinking and behavioral processes that underlie entrepreneurship – such as being opportunity oriented, taking calculated risks, and striving to change and improve the status quo. Thus, the development team practices *intrapreneurship* – the pursuit of entrepreneurial behaviors by individuals within an existing organization. As *intrapreneurs*, the development team members look for new and innovative opportunities to improve products and/or services and to expand the scope of marketing and

operations to a larger customer base (Pinchot, 1985; Kourilsky, 1998; Kourilsky & Walstad, 2000).

The development team has a strong affinity for the initiator (or initiator team) and is deeply committed to the vision the initiator team is pursuing. It is the entrepreneurial development team that will apply their entrepreneurial expertise and attitudes to expand the scope, size, and market of the educational venture and take the enterprise to its next level of growth. Although the members of the entrepreneurial development team may not themselves be the initiators for the venture at hand, the boundaries between the initiator and development team levels are "porous," and development team members often evolve into the subsequent initiators of other ventures.

At the entrepreneurial behavior level of the pyramid, among the key differences exhibited by the not-for-profit and for profit sectors are their approaches to and emphases on the issue of "scaling up". With due regard for minimizing impact on the integrity of the social mission, growth is generally perceived by the development team as almost an axiomatic requirement for an educational entrepreneurship "for profit" that wants to continue its success. Although not as directly vulnerable to the "scale or be scuttled!" school of thought, not-for-profit development teams are not immune to the lure of scaling up. Potential pressure from the community and from funders – coupled with the philanthropic urge to cast an ever-wider net of social benefits and the appeal of potential efficiencies of scale – can argue quite persuasively for expansion. The committed not-for-profit development team, however, stringently trades off these arguments for scaling up against the potential costs and risks in areas such as mission, quality, reputation dilution, over standardization, and infrastructure strain (Taylor, Dees, & Emerson, 2002). They also must take into account one of the primary constraints on scaling in not-for-profits – access to funding specifically for growth. Finally, public sector development teams generally are limited to "guerilla" intrapreneurship tactics to pursue any kind of growth activity. In addition to the expected budget and regulatory issues, they face constraints imposed by jurisdictional boundaries that demarcate the geographical and demographic limits on units of government.

"Entrepreneurism." Neither the initiator level nor the development team level of the pyramid could exist and function successfully without the third level of the pyramid – which carries the label "entrepreneurism" and whose inhabitants are referred to as the "constituency." Here, the word "constituency" does not carry its normal political connotations of voters or the electorate. Rather, "constituency" in this context carries a connotation of overall support or "buy-in." It is intended to refer to the members of the general public who encourage the objectives and the processes of entrepreneurship and entrepreneurial behaviors – and believe they are stakeholders in and beneficiaries of the resulting economic and social outcomes. In the for profit

segment of the private sector, the constituency plays a key role by expressing their political support for decision-makers and policies that create an environment conducive to the emergence and successful operation of entrepreneurial educational ventures whose outcomes are perceived as socially desirable. With respect to the not-for-profit and public sectors, the constituency weighs in by expressing their support for policies and decision-makers that preserve and enhance the tax incentive structure for not-for-profit organizations – and that facilitate the ability of government units to overcome creatively some of the limitations imposed by the obligations and boundaries of their jurisdictions and demographic charters.

3. The Growth of Conditions Favoring Educational Entrepreneurship

The characteristics most highly valued in educational leaders at a particular point in history are, by definition, shaped by the context of the time. If "educational entrepreneurship" has salience in education today, it is attributable to social, political, and economic changes in education that favor it. Since the Civil War, public education has been considered a right and "public" requirement for all citizens up through age eighteen (Tyack, 1974). Before that period, most schools were privately run institutions that were accessible primarily to the children of those privileged either socially or by religious affiliation. The political goal of assimilating large numbers of new immigrants was paralleled and reinforced by the growing belief that schools should teach people the necessary job skills to become effective and productive members of society. The advent of "the common school" carried with it acceptance of the notions that every citizen (not just parents) should be taxed to support schooling and that the taxing authority should be the school provider. Proponents brought about a widespread system of public education that formed the basis of what has evolved into today's educational environment.

Almost 15,000 school districts currently operate across the country under the auspices of local and state governments, which also represent the primary source of funding for their member schools. In addition, the Federal government plays a small, but significant role in subsidizing educational resources for selected groups of students who are underserved – low-income, special education, physically handicapped, and others.

Education policy makers (and those who support them) have traditionally believed in the *positive externalities* of education – the benefits that accrue to society as a whole from an individual's education (beyond those benefits that accrue directly to the individual over her or his lifetime) (Heyne, 2000). From an economics perspective, the aggregate individual demand for education was believed to under-represent society's overall demand for education of its participants ("private market failure"). Policy-makers therefore feared that not enough of the good (i.e., education) would be produced (and consumed) to meet society's demand if the production and consumption decisions were left purely to individual demands in the market (Kourilsky, 2001).

Recognition of the desire to produce more of a public good such as education and to encourage more consumption of that good, however, need not necessarily lead either to a monopoly structure of public provision or in theory to any direct public provision of the good. If the general public, whose voice is expressed by the political process, believes that not enough of a "desirable" good would be produced and consumed in a pure market setting, government more typically intervenes by trying to work through the market rather than by absorbing the production process into a publicly-run effort. Government usually attempts to influence markets by targeting the supply/production side, the demand/consumption side, or some combination of the two. For example, government can incentivize suppliers to produce more of a good through subsidies or other means of increasing the goods' profitability. Alternatively, government can make it easier for consumers to have access to goods or services through transfer payments or income redistribution.[3]

In the case of education, government can remedy the problems of perceived private market inadequacy or failure by reducing the private cost/ price of schooling to citizens. In cases where the government elects to pursue the more drastic intervention of compelling certain levels of consumption (e.g., compulsory education through high school), political and socioeconomic considerations often dictate that government also make the compulsory schooling available at a reduced price or as a zero-price service. (The argument differs only in degree when schooling is not compulsory.) It can reduce the price by increasing the supply of schooling through direct provision and/or by contracting with other providers. Government also can increase the demand for schooling by providing parents of children with the financial means to purchase schooling and/or by imposing statutory requirements. Governments throughout the world employ wide variations on these basic options (including co-payment by parents). In the United States, government evolved into the principal funder and direct provider of free (to the family) schooling. "Public education" became an integral service and near monopoly of the public sector – and in the case of the United States, a compulsory service provided primarily by state and local governments.[4]

What factors, then, are spurring today's departure from these historical perspectives and the growing belief that various forms of market competition should be introduced into the domain previously reserved primarily for public sector supplied education? Furthermore, how are these factors being manifested?

---

3.   For a further discussion of this point, see Kourilsky & Dickneider, 1988; Kourilsky, 2001.

3.1. Increasing Publicly Expressed Dissatisfaction

The public is increasingly dissatisfied with the public sector in general. Results of national polls indicate that only 3 in 10 U.S. citizens think government operates for the benefit of everyone. National surveys further reveal public perceptions of government planning as "inadequate" and of government program outcomes as "highly problematic" (Hula, 1990; Murphy, Gilmer, Weise, & Page, 1998).

In addition, surveys over the past few decades have highlighted the trend toward declining public confidence in their public schools, in part because of increases in the individual, personal consequences of a good or bad education.[5] The proportion of people who possessed a "great deal" or "quite a lot" of confidence in public schools dropped from 58% to 36% from 1973 to 1999. Over that same time period the percentage of respondents who said they had "very little confidence or none" grew from 11% to 26% (Public Agenda, 1973-1999).[6] A further marker for the public's apparent confidence issues with respect to public schooling is the steady increase in home schooling recorded during the last two decades.[7]

Kourilsky and Walstad (2000) have studied the opinions and beliefs of students, teachers, and business leaders to determine the degree of alignment between education goals and student preparation. All three groups believe that schools are not delivering the necessary curriculum for students either to "make a job" for themselves effectively in the future as venture initiators or to "take a job" successfully as employees of a venture. Parents also hold this same view, especially with respect to at-risk populations (Kourilsky and Kourilsky, 1999).

The topic of education is identified regularly by Americans as one of their top priorities in opinion surveys. Gallup surveys in May and June of 2001, for

---

4.   Certainly, the private not-for-profit and for profit sectors have long played a role in aspects of public education. However, this role has been limited in the past either to the initiation of self-contained private schools and educational service organizations or to vendor support enterprises providing products primarily in three areas – 1) creating and disseminating curricula in the form of textbooks and instructional materials, 2) providing goods such as materials, computers, and supplies, and 3) offering non-instructional services such as food or transportation.

5.   Increasingly, what individuals know and can do ("human capital") is a key determinant of their personal "socioeconomic horizons" and their capacity for social and economic impact as well as the overall economic and social well-being of the regions, states, or countries in which they live. This fact has fuelled significant increases in aggregate and per capita demand for schooling to levels that are very difficult to supply and/or finance through traditional models of provision and funding.

6.   Public Agenda, a not-for-profit organization, has polled Americans on education related issues for decades.

7.   The National Home Education Institute estimates that between 1.5 and 1.9 million K-12 students were homeschooled during the 2000-2001 school year, and those numbers are growing between 7 and 15% per year (http://www.nheri.org).

example, showed that education was the top or one of the top issues in America. Sixty-nine percent (69%) of respondents rated education "extremely important," the highest rating choice in the survey, a percentage that ranked education above other major national issues including a "patient's bill of rights" and "keeping America prosperous."

3.2. Increasing Reliance on Multiple Sources of Revenue

Inherent limits to funding of public educational institutions have forced educational leaders to pursue a variety of nontraditional revenue streams, including revenue sources not directly linked to the public school system (e.g. educational partnerships in the juvenile justice and health areas), not-for-profit educational philanthropy, and for profit education businesses. Examples include business support of private schools, public school foundations, employer funding of adult education, investment banking targeted to education businesses, and developer fees for new school construction. The pursuit of these alternative revenue streams has in turn fostered the creation and growth of both new ventures and new forms of ventures in the not-for-profit and for profit sectors of the economy.

3.3. Changing Organizational Frameworks: from Centralized Public Models to Decentralized Market Models

Just as exclusively public financing has given way to mixed financing from a variety of sources, exclusively public provision of publicly financed education services is giving way to educators employed through new blends of public, not-for-profit, and for profit organizations. These new organizations, which in part reflect the "market" seeking to address perceived shortfalls in both the productivity and the quality of public education, provide direct services to students via contracts with public educational organizations – or charge private fees directly to students. The new firms also are providing desired services to existing schools, colleges, and universities through various forms of alliances and vendor contracts.

3.4. Increasing Inter-penetration by Education Service Providers of Historically Protected Markets

Geographic segmentation for purposes of organization, control, and delivery of educational services is accommodating increasingly to a market blend that crosses traditional geographic boundaries of educational services. Charter schools, magnet schools, public/private voucher programs, inter-district transfers and open enrollment policies exist alongside and inter-penetrate across the fixed attendance boundaries of neighborhood public schools. Distance-delivered programs at universities are crossing state boundaries in which they are chartered as well as boundaries of regional accrediting agencies. As political and technical barriers to entry fall, new "virtual" education businesses providing on-line education, such as Virtual High School, increasingly are able to serve students across attendance area, district, state, and national boundaries.

3.5. Changing Relationships Between the 'Policy End' and the 'Operation End' as Educational Organizations Move from Compliance to Performance

Direction from the "top" of traditional (largely public sector) education organizations has shifted from enforcing compliance in providing uniform educational services to creating incentives for improving student performance. Especially in K-12 and community college systems, the federal and state governments are seeking increasingly to tie government funding to student academic performance while increasing the flexibility of laws and regulations that require compliance with uniform procedures. The same is true for state licensing programs in teacher education, in which local providers have increased "accountability" for the performance levels of graduates in tandem with greater flexibility in program design. Similarly, as they are being held more accountable for improved student performance, educators providing direct services to students also are gaining more latitude in determining how they will provide services. As a consequence, new education ventures (and new programs created by existing education enterprises) that promise increased student performance are gaining more acceptance as viable alternatives for public school "customers" than in the past.

3.6. Increasing Reliance on Technology for Service Delivery, Organization, and Operation

Rapid developments in technology are driving down dramatically the cost of "handling information" in existing organizations, but they also are influencing significantly the form and creation of newer education ventures. Communication technology platform advances and interactive learning paradigm enhancements are enabling the evolution of new types of education enterprises and fundamentally altering the organization and service mix of many existing education institutions and firms. A number of education firms have emerged in recent decades whose core mission entails some form of "e-learning." For example, currently twelve states have established online high school programs; twenty-five states allow the creation of "cyber" charter schools; and thirty-two states have e-learning initiatives underway (*Education Week*, May 9, 2002).

4. Education as an Industry Today

Although schools, colleges, and universities have been a common part of life for centuries, the term "education industry" has come into common usage only within the last ten years. When the term "industry" is used in this context, it usually connotes a wide amalgamation of firms, government agencies, associations, foundations, and other organizations that are closely affiliated or aligned with a common area of interest, as in "medical industry," "defense industry," and the "automobile industry." Until recently the term "education industry" was unnecessary, because "schools, colleges, and universities" sufficed. However, several forces over the last 20 years have led to the creation of newer, less visible organizations also within the education industry that are separate and distinct from traditional schools, colleges, and universities.

Public and traditional not-for-profit educational institutions in the U.S. (a system of about 15,000 school districts within which are located about 125 thousand schools plus about 3500 public and private colleges and universities) are responsible for about $750 billion in annual business activity in the United States. These institutions are being supplemented by a growing number of not-for-profit and for profit private sector educational ventures. Of these, at least 1000 with five or more employees are largely for-profit education ventures, with this newer, more narrowly defined segment currently generating something over $100 billion in annual business activity. [8] (These numbers may well reflect some overlapping of business activity, because of the likelihood of "double counting" when, for example, a public institution contracts with a for profit education business.)

The newer education businesses that characterize the education industry are much more focused and specialized in the goods and services they provide. The number and variety of narrowly focused educational organizations are growing, with each organization seeking to pursue niches in the education market place. The core business of Futurekids, for example, is providing teacher training in classroom applications of computers; the Chicago Teachers Union has become the first labor organization in the nation to launch a graduate school for K-12 educators; Sylvan Learning provides tutoring in reading and math; EDUCATE LA provides Los Angeles County parents and

---

8.   Based on analysis of firms tracked by Eduventures, Inc. See http://www.eduventures.com.

families with a centralized source for education related programs and services in addition to producing the interactive Web CD EDUCATE LA Resource Directory; Parents In Charge (PIC) is a not-for-profit dedicated to informing and organizing the public with respect to the problems and possibilities in K-12 education and school reform. Edison Schools comes closest to providing a comprehensive service, but it markets only one form of comprehensive service.

Because the education industry is evolving and growing so rapidly, definitions and taxonomies of the *categories* of firms that make up the education industry are themselves also evolving. While traditional categories of schools are based on the ages of the student and to a lesser extent the character, curriculum, and overall objectives of the schooling entity – e.g., day care, elementary schools, community colleges, doctoral granting universities – the firms of the education industry currently are more readily categorized by their primary markets (three) and core mission focus (four).

4.1. Primary Markets

Primary markets include pre and K-12 education (the principal focus of this paper), corporate education, and post-secondary education. Youth education ventures and institutions, including the infrastructure and service organizations that support them, are the primary enterprises that address the largest of the three primary markets, pre and K-12. Providing functions that include childcare, pre and K-12 learning, and services for students with special needs, the for profits alone that are addressing this market account for over $50 billion of annual education industry revenues.[9]

4.2. Core Mission Focus

The core focus of most enterprises in the education industry falls into one of four broad categories: education delivery, content, infrastructure, and services. Those whose core mission is *delivery* provide bundles of learning delivery education functions for students, ranging from traditional and specialty school

---

9. The distinction between pre and K-12 education and the other two primary markets is clearer than the distinction between those other two markets themselves, largely because of the demarcation of age. The differentiation between post-secondary and corporate markets is based more on the type of course provided than on the age of the student. Post-secondary education typically refers to traditional, credit bearing, semester-long (or quarter-long) courses leading to formal academic degrees, e.g., Associates, Bachelors, and Masters degrees. On the other hand, corporate training usually refers to shorter, non-credit bearing courses of instruction that typically do not lead to academic degrees and that may or may not lead to training or continuing education certificates based on satisfactory completion.

instruction to corporate training to childcare. Most education delivery organizations and companies specialize in one of the three primary markets. Examples of pre and K-12 education delivery ventures include KinderCare Learning Centers and Bright Horizons Family Solutions (childcare), Edison Schools and Nobel Learning Centers (K-12), and Aspen Education Group and Ombudsman (specialty schools). Examples of education delivery businesses in post-secondary education are Apollo Group and DeVry, and in corporate training are Global Knowledge and Learning Tree.

Organizations whose core mission is *content* frequently include enterprises that publish curriculum materials and (in the pre and K-12 primary market) materials for testing student knowledge of the curriculum. (An example of the latter is EduTest, the online assessment and accountability division of Lightspan, Inc.). Firms specializing in electronic learning or e-learning provide a relatively large fraction of publishing for the corporate training primary market. Firms in this area often develop software-driven training programs that corporate employees can take at on-site computer terminals or at terminals located near to where they work. The actual delivery of the learning curriculum can vary from local mass storage based implementations to distance learning implementations across proprietary networks and the Web.

Infrastructure is a label applied to the core mission of ventures – such as Blackboard and WebCT – that provide various forms of (largely technological) support for teaching and learning (including distance learning). These enterprises may sell (or donate) to schools and colleges products ranging across computer hardware, networking equipment, desktop and server software, and web-based applications as well as staff training in how to use educational support technology. These firms also may manufacture and/or distribute a variety of products, equipment, supplies, and curriculum materials to schools and colleges.

Not-for-profit and for profit entities focusing on *educational services*, such as National Teacher Training Institute (focusing on classroom Internet use) and Tutor.com, are differentiated from *education delivery* organizations in that their core mission is to provide support functions that assist and evaluate other firms in the delivery of primary learning content and assist and evaluate students in the acquisition of learning content. Their activities can range over a spectrum that includes specialty education services, professional development for instructors, curriculum and standards consulting, measurement and accountability services, student tutoring and student test preparation services, and student testing and assessment functions.

The various types of firms described above constitute (directly and indirectly) the vast majority of educating enterprises, i.e., those organizations that by themselves or with other ventures, produce the education goods and services that make up the education industry. In addition to these direct producers, three other types of not-for-profit and for profit organizations are key contributors to the private sectors of the education industry: *banks and venture capital institutions* that specialize in investing in education; *information firms* that provide to clients detailed, current, and sophisticated levels of data and analysis about the performance and prospects of individual firms and collections of firms within the education industry; and education industry affiliated *professional organizations* whose membership share interests and information with respect to various areas of the education industry. Examples of these organizations abound, including Sprout and Warburg Pincus (investing in education), Eduventures and Knowledge Quest Ventures (information), and the Association of Educational Practitioners and Providers (professional membership).

Of course, the vast majority of these firms (or at least their major K-12 divisions) was created within the last generation and, by definition, was formed by entrepreneurs. One might assert, therefore, that educational entrepreneurship "has already arrived" in K-12 education. To do so, however, would be to shortchange both the concept of educational entrepreneurship and its potential for K-12 education, as would focusing on any one of the three sectors to the exclusion of the other two.

5. Inter-Sector Comparative Advantages

Based on the trends influencing the education industry and the apparent trajectory along which it is evolving today, it is clear that not-for-profits and for profits from the private sector will continue to seek out and enter spaces in K-12 education. If only by virtue of aggregate economic activity, K-12 education is a three-sector domain, i.e., made up of firms whose sector locations, all else equal, provide them certain advantages, opportunities, and constraints.[10] How might the relative advantages of the sectors be leveraged in a coordinated fashion to pursue the greatest amount of educational reform and learning improvement in our schools?

---

10. A number of studies have been conducted which address the interplay of the characteristics of firms in different economic sectors in particular policy areas as well as inter-sector collaboration in those policy areas. See for example: The Conference Board, Council on Foundations, Independent Sector, National Academy of Public Administration, National Alliance of Business, & National Governors Association. (2000); "Changing roles, changing relationships: The new challenge for business, non-profit organizations, and government"; Rosenau, P. V. (Ed.). (2000). *Public-Private Partnerships.* Cambridge, MA: The MIT Press; and Weisbrod, B. A. (1977). Toward a theory of the voluntary nonprofit sector in a three-sector economy, *The Voluntary Non-Profit Sector* (pp. 51-71). Lexington, MA: Lexington Books.

A helpful analytical lens through which to view the issues just raised is an adaptation of a familiar one from the intellectual toolkit of the economist. What are the respective *comparative advantages* (in both the social mission sense and the economic productivity sense) in the K-12 learning "market" of the public sector, the not-for-profit private sector, and the for profit private sector?

Technically, <u>absolute advantage</u> refers to the ability of a producer to provide a good or service *with fewer resources* than do other producers. On the other hand, <u>comparative advantage</u> refers to the ability of a producer to provide a good or service *at a lower opportunity* cost than do other producers (Kourilsky & Dickneider, 1988). For example, when George Herman "Babe" Ruth began playing for the New York Yankees, he was thought to be the best hitter and pitcher on the team. That is, Babe Ruth had an <u>absolute</u> advantage in <u>both</u> hitting and pitching. The coaches would have liked him to do both, but pitchers cannot play every day to allow their arms to rest between pitching games. The coaches decided instead that Babe should not pitch because they believed the opportunity cost of using him as a pitcher was too high. There were two reasons for this conclusion. In the first place, although other members of the team were fine pitchers, no one could touch Babe at hitting. In the second place, if Babe's arm held up well enough for him to pitch even in every fourth game (for example), he would still warm the bench during the other three games. The opportunity cost of Babe's pitching was the hitting the team would sacrifice during the games when Babe was not allowed to pitch. Because Babe had a comparative advantage in hitting while others had a comparative advantage in pitching (even though Babe had an absolute advantage in both), the coaches ended up with a more successful team by having Babe <u>specialize</u> in hitting while others specialized in pitching.

The above example has an analogue in the education industry. Just because a sector (public, private not-for-profit, or private for profit) may have an *absolute* advantage in a given area of education reform, it does not follow necessarily that it has a *comparative* advantage in that same area. Each district (and/or each school within a district, depending on the level of decentralization) ultimately will have to make its own decisions about the best division of "educational" labor for meeting their learning and administrative responsibilities towards the students in their respective jurisdictions and for pursuing educational reform in particular areas. It is useful to that decision-making process, however, to consider what each sector, historically and potentially, can bring to the table in the way of comparative advantages with respect to particular functions. In fact, serious discussion and analysis is merited about the potential of improving the quality of the whole "package" of educational reform in the education industry by strategic leveraging of the comparative advantages of each of its candidate producer sectors, i.e. by pursuing a strategy of multisectorism. We continue below with an attempt to initiate that dialogue by highlighting selected areas of potential comparative advantage within each of the sectors. [11]

5.1. K-12 Government (Public) Sector

The government or public sector has the benefit of access to tax revenues and has the responsibility for assuring minimally acceptable levels of schooling to all eligible children regardless of social, demographic, or economic background. Additionally, it makes and modifies the rules of commerce that govern education firms in all three sectors. Equity for all is, perhaps, its core value. One can argue for the comparative advantage of the public school sector in several key areas: core learning, social justice initiatives, and holistic anchoring of the student. The public schools manifest a comparative advantage with respect to their historical responsibilities for the delivery of K-12 core learning the foundational knowledge and skills in areas that include reading, language arts, mathematics, and basic science. As creative and innovative as private not-for-profit and private for profit suppliers might be with respect to K-12 core learning, they in the end still constitute a *market* with all that implies – free to come and go, free to change what they teach and to whom they teach with the vagaries of philanthropic funding and missions and the oscillations of supply, demand, and the general economic health of the economy. Because of the potential for significant damage to students as a result of supply variations or especially of supply interruptions, K-12 core learning is an example of a class of functions for which in-house production can be argued to be preferable (Hirsch, 1991). Public schools thus have the structural advantage with respect to reliable delivery over the long-term of K-12 core learning and – with that advantage – a strong argument for their retention in-house of their historical responsibilities in that area.

Government operated public schools also exhibit an advantage with respect to the pursuit of social justice in education. Public schools are in a better position to have relationships with and understand the unmet needs and inequitable access profiles of their community constituencies that are underserved. Additionally, their scale, public monopoly powers, and their close linkage to government funding positions them more strategically to be the delivery agents for broad government reform initiatives in the area of social justice. Private not-for-profit and for profit enterprises certainly can and do engage in both minor and major initiatives for the enhancement of social

---

11. Voucher plans are outside the scope of this paper's discussion. Voucher plans might of course impact the choice of educational organization or institution within sectors. However, such plans would not affect materially the intrinsic <u>comparative</u> advantages of the not-for-profit sector, the for profit sector, and the public sector. Similarly, home schooling also is outside the scope of this paper.

justice in learning. However, the public school systems have the advantages of structure, reach, and knowledge of their surrounding communities.

Finally – particularly for the underserved – the public schools are in the best position to act as the anchor point for the student as a whole, as each student makes her/his way through the K-12 school system. Private schools also are capable of performing such functions, of course, but the ones that do so typically tend to be beyond the socioeconomic reach of students in underserved communities and sometimes are beyond the reach of students from even moderate socioeconomic environments. For the majority of students, the public schools retain the advantage with respect to the capacity for being the learner's homebase – their primary physical point of contact for learning as well as the nexus of information and functions which track the student's entire academic profile and provide equitable guidance and career counseling. Some readers may be tempted to argue that the public school system's well-publicized failures in guidance and counseling are legion. Without debating the merits of that assertion, it is really beside the point we are making. Trying to achieve better performance in this area certainly is an important public school reform issue. However, there is, for example, no evidence or long-term track record that convincingly supports the assertion that private not-for-profit or for profit enterprises have an advantage over urban public school educators in working with poor students of color (Farrell, Johnson, Jones, & Sapp, 1994). Public schools still have the intrinsic comparative advantage in terms of their capacity to deliver in this area for the underserved and for low and moderately low socioeconomic students.

5.2. K-12 Private Not-For-Profit Sector

Highlighting the comparative advantages of the public sector in turn helps bring into focus some of the intrinsic comparative advantages respectively for the not-for-profit and for profit private sectors. Stated simply, the not-for-profit sector has access to the "hearts" of individuals and organizations that value K-12 education. This sector provides the philanthropic and tax-advantaged means and incentives for them to apply land, labor, and capital (human, social, fiscal, and physical) to K-12 education "causes." The "gaps" left by government provision are first filled by this sector. (Just as governments respond to "private market failure," not-for-profits respond to "public market failure.") Tens of thousands of voluntary, "cause-oriented" K-12 organizations already provide an exceptionally wide range of public good and service "needs" that are not provided or only partially provided by the public sector. Filling unmet social needs is perhaps the core value of this sector.

5.3. K-12 Private For Profit Sector

The ability of the for profit sector to identify market opportunities (and, often, creative ideas to address those opportunities), access investment capital, build compelling and innovative business models, and successfully sell their goods and services lies at the heart of its comparative advantage. Examples of goods and services from for profit providers can be found across the full range of the K-12 domain, but their existence is very closely linked to their perceived value in the marketplace. When educational entrepreneurs (as we defined them early in this paper) pursue the social mission of education in the for profit sector, that mission must always be integrated appropriately with the fundamental efficiency objectives that are perhaps the values closest to the core of this sector.

The for profit sector's "market test" is reflected in goods and services sold to households, e.g., encyclopedias, as well as in goods and services sold to other educationally oriented businesses, e.g., instructional objectives and testing services. The business-to-customer vs. business-to-business ("B to C" vs. "B to B") distinction is important here, because such a large proportion of potential business customers in the education industry are public educational enterprises. In many B to B instances, for profit firms concentrate on niches and customers in the public sector. Many of these target customers in the public sector find that the cost/value proposition and scale economies of the for profit firm yield a product or service which is more competitive than that which could be provided within the average size school district (6 schools, $23M annual operating budget).

The economies of scale argument, however, must be applied with some caution. For example, a common assumption of the founders of aspiring educational management organizations (EMOs) – such as the initiators of Edison Schools – has been that national expansion would be accompanied by significant economies of scale and corresponding financial growth for the company. However, research has established that the reality of the industry economics does not support such assumptions. In fact, it has been demonstrated that the decline in per pupil costs levels out at about 6000 students or less and that expansion beyond this level actually begins to manifest diseconomies of scale (Andrews, Duncombe, and Yinger, 2002).

5.4. Comparative Advantage Arenas of the Private Sectors

Given today's educational landscape, the comparative advantage arenas of the private not-for-profit and for profit sectors have large regions of overlap. Among the important considerations that ultimately determine the not-for-profit or for profit "tilt" of any particular venture in these areas is the character of the funding/investment sources to which it is most likely to appeal. In other words, for any particular instance of a social mission oriented educational venture, the affinity towards the not-for-profit sector relative to the for profit sector will be determined often by the agendas of the candidate funding communities. For example, if an educational venture were to appeal strongly to the philanthropic community's drive to fill gaps consistent with social need, it might experience a strong draw to become part of the not-for-profit sector of the economy. On the other hand, ventures that are capable of achieving simultaneously both educational social outcomes and profits would be more likely to appeal to funders in the private investment community and might find the financing currents tending to carry them towards the structure of a for profit enterprise.

Additionally, the "politics of acceptance" will play a role in the form the venture eventually takes. The educational community tends to greet for profits with reflex mistrust of their commitment to social objectives – abetted by the not infrequent perception of profit as a residual or surplus that threatens to "siphon off" resources that otherwise could be used for enhancing educational outcomes. This automatic "negative press" is substantially more muted for not-for-profits. However, they too can expect to encounter resistance unless they work to secure buy-in, particularly from teachers who perceive a displacement threat and from the unions who represent them.

With these contrasting considerations in mind, we proceed to highlight some of the key areas of the educational industry in which either private sector may contribute advantageously to enhance the potential for educational reform. For the private sectors taken as a whole, two important areas of comparative advantage are specialty education services and new school alternatives (such as charter schools). [12]

5.5. Specialty Education Services

Specialty education services build upon and enhance the core K-12 education functions but typically do not have the primary responsibility for delivery of

---

12. Non-educational support services are not included in this discussion because they are so peripheral to the underlying spirit of education as a social mission. Nevertheless, it should be noted that with its profile of competing ventures providing greater service variety and customization, higher efficiency, reduced costs, and easy switching to more favorable vendor relationships, the private for profit sector's advantages in providing support services for non-educational areas such as school transportation, food, and building maintenance have long been recognized by the public school system. In fact, it was reported in 1995 that the contracting out by public schools of services such as these – which are clearly distinct from the direct functions of delivering learning to students – already had reached estimated levels exceeding 30% of school transportation, 30% of cafeteria operations, and 10% of cleaning, repair, and maintenance (NSBA, 1995).

the core. As such, these services are especially amenable to the creativity of the private sector marketplace as their delivery is relatively unfettered (in contrast to that of the core K-12 functions) by the constraints of regulated implementation procedures. Additionally, to the extent that their focus is on enrichment of the K-12 core learning areas rather than on the core areas themselves, they may encourage a more accommodating response from public school teachers and teacher unions.

Private sector provision of the middle and late 1990s already had made its influence known in a number of specialty areas including vocational education, substitute teacher bureaus, and services for at-risk children (Beales & O'Leary, 1993; Thomas, 1996). Private provision further has expanded to include instructional support in areas such as testing, drivers education, instructional technology, professional development, pre-school and after-school programs, and instructional camps – and supplementary curricular areas such as foreign languages and science. A Berlitz International language contract with a New Jersey elementary school and Science Encounter alliances with Maryland school districts are characteristic respectively of private sector relationships with public schools to teach foreign languages and to provide supplementary science education options such as a mobile science laboratories and summer "booster" workshops for science teachers.

5.6. Start Up Charter Schools

One of the most visible components of the *new school alternatives area* is the charter school arena, whose participants most often are the product of public and not-for-profit (and, sometimes, for-profit) relationships. Political and legal exposure considerations – rather than statutory limitations – were responsible in the main for the rarity with which school districts had in the past contracted out educational services to providers from the not-for-profit and for profit sectors. That situation was transformed by the advent of charter school legislation, which breached the historically "exclusive" school oversight rights of districts and opened the door for "non-district" initiation and operation of public schools. Typically taking the form of not-for-profit corporations – often with specialized objectives in mind – charter schools' reliance on parent or guardian choice for student enrollment immediately drew the attention of entrepreneurial thinkers and venture-initiating social entrepreneurs in the educational market. The operating environment for these innovation-oriented educational enterprises was much more favorable towards the contracting of services both to the not-for-profit and to the for profit sectors of the economy, and both producers and consumers moved rapidly into the market vacuum.

With their genesis firmly rooted in the desire to facilitate creative approaches to the schooling of our youth, the charter school segment was essentially "given birth" to catalyze and nurture innovation and change. This "birthright" is reflected in a comparative advantage for implementing educational "laboratories" in which to test out best practices and alternative approaches for delivering learning and for the administration of that delivery. One potentially seminal outgrowth of this charter "laboratory" environment was the concept of teacher cooperatives.

5.7. Teacher Cooperatives

Teacher cooperatives – in a sense a hybrid development from both the private (not-for-profit and for profit) and the public sectors – have the potential for combining a number of the advantages of both sectors for the delivery of education in the K-12 arena. Although teacher cooperatives constitute a tiny fraction of the nation's teachers, the phenomenon is one of the most provocative and visibly evolving trends in educational entrepreneurship.

Beales (1994) describes the members of teacher cooperatives as professional educator teams that provide their services to schools or other organizations on a contract basis. In their most common manifestations today, small groups of teachers who are oriented towards social entrepreneurship are organizing themselves into professional partnership practices. These partnerships to date have taken the form most frequently of cooperatives, legally structured in ways that are most appropriate to the statutory and administrative context of the local school districts and states within which the partnerships are establishing contracting relationships. EdVisions, a "teacher-as-owner" Minnesota cooperative formed in 1994, was an early example of this innovation. EdVisions took on the contractual responsibility for running both the learning program and the daily operation of the Minnesota New Country School, a not-for-profit charter school. The partner teacher-owners were completely in charge of the school's pedagogical decisions and materials, assignments and performance evaluation, and hiring and compensation processes (Dirkswager, 2002). Until recently, teacher cooperatives coalesced around a variety of themes including subject matter (e.g. music), learning methods (e.g. phonics), unit of a course (e.g. U.S. Civil War), targeted student groups (e.g. gifted students) and teaching approaches such as computer-assisted learning (Wenger, 1994; Yelich, 1994; Murphy, Gilmer, Weise, & Page, 1998).

Members of teacher cooperatives today act as social entrepreneurs, who not only may transform the way education is delivered but also may have a profound impact on teaching as a career choice. Like other entrepreneurs, these teachers are now "making a job" rather than just "taking a job." Members of teacher cooperatives no longer think of themselves as employees. They have the mindset of owners who recognize opportunities, marshal resources, create ventures (such as their cooperatives), are "customer"-driven, and are willing to take risks in order to implement their educational visions. Teacher cooperatives also reinforce the "professionalization" of teaching by presenting alternative career development paths "within teaching." These paths support educators' continuing to practice and grow in the art and science of learning and instruction rather than forcing teachers who wish to advance their careers to move "upstairs" into administration or "outside" into lateral career options. In a variety of ways, then, attributes of teacher cooperatives incentivize change and efficiency. On the other hand, members of teacher cooperatives also tap into the advantages of the public sector in that they themselves typically emerge from the ranks of public school teachers. As such, they benefit from "insider status" which enables them to connect and integrate more readily with the institutional continuity and "student anchoring" functions of the public schools, the various school and community constituencies, and the public school's core learning agendas and requirements. By combining these advantages from both the private (not-for-profit and for profit) and the public sectors, teacher cooperatives may well enjoy a significant comparative advantage in the modeling of alternative delivery structures for K-12 education.

Attendant with the various current and potential transformational trends within the education industry, there is a risk of unintended collateral damage: the deprofessionalization of the teacher. Both market innovation and technology innovation are giving rise to classroom instruction delivery products at a dizzying pace. One would hope such innovation trends would represent a force that can be harnessed to accrue benefits for teacher professional development as well as for student learning outcomes and for the education industry in general. Unfortunately, a deluge of well-marketed products is homing in on the current testing and accountability trends nationwide. The "curb appeals" of these products often are based largely on assertions (frequently unsubstantiated) about improving student performance on newly mandated standardized tests. Administrative and parent decision-makers are feeling increasing market and regulatory pressure to adopt such programs as "uniform approaches" to help district schools and alternative new schools avoid the undesirable consequences of failing to achieve student increases on accountability instruments.

The result already is an uncomfortable number of classrooms in which most of the student instruction is dictated and/or delivered by canned content and technology products. The curriculum product – rather than the teacher – tends to be seen as the locus of "knowledge" and "understanding" and of the ability to deliver both to the students. The curriculum products are positioned as "what matters," and the teachers often are relegated largely to custodial roles. If this trend were to continue unabated, it arguably could lead to the inadvertent deprofessionalization of teaching: adopted products of unknown quality and impact would control much of classroom instruction by fiat; teachers would have substantially less opportunity to adapt classroom pedagogical approaches to the varying individual learning styles and requirements of the students or – more generally – to bring their professional expertise and experience to bear on the instructional decision-making that is key to classroom learning; and the teacher role would be reduced effectively to that of a product caretaker – a "replaceable" function that could just as easily be fulfilled by less trained, less experienced, and less expensive paraprofessionals.

Deprofessionalization risks similar to the ones just described are likely to be faced in all three sectors as we go forward. Compounding these risks is a tendency on the part of broad segments of the general public and many decision-makers to underestimate the complicated trade-offs and sophisticated intellectual requirements of real education and instructional decision-making. The determined march of innovation in education will require vigilance of equal commitment from all three sectors to maintain and enhance the "professionalism" of teaching and to ensure that educational decision-making is adequately informed and guided by that professionalism. The repercussions of mistakes in this area can be quite harsh, potentially compromising student learning capacity in entire subject areas or even across subject areas for years to come (if not for the rest of their lives).

6. Conclusion: Beyond Comparative Advantages – to Covisionary Multisectoral Synergies

Significant illustrations of entrepreneurship and entrepreneurial thinking both can be found and can emerge in (and among) any sector of an economy. Such emergence depends on the venture governance incentives in place and the degree to which ventures can work with and around their portfolio of constraints for the implementation of their vision and mission.

In the not-for-profit private sector, the lion's share of the focus is on the educational social vision and mission – how best to achieve impact in the targeted areas of social need (but with no obligation to provide minimal levels of service across an entire jurisdiction, unlike the public or government sector). Organizations within this sector strive to attain educational outcomes for K-12 youth that are viewed both as desirable and as acceptable levels of accomplishment by donors, organization associates, and society.

In the for profit private sector, although the educational social mission is still key (as it is for the other two sectors by our introductory definition), it cannot unilaterally drive all decisions. The pursuit of the social mission does have to be balanced responsibly against the economic obligations of the venture to generate an acceptable level of financial return for founders, private investors, and possibly public investors (in the case of a public corporation.)

In the public arena, the educational social mission is nominally center stage (as in the not-for-profit sector) with the additional imperative to provide minimally acceptable levels of service for the relevant governmental jurisdiction(s). Across all sectors, the social mission also is constrained in practice and must find an acceptable balance with respect to the realities of funding, politics, regulations, markets, and "turf" constraints.

We have deliberately used the term "comparative advantage" in our consideration of the relative sector advantages with respect to firms and organizations in K-12 education. Our intention was to dispose aggressively of the notion that any one sector somehow enjoys a "universal" natural advantage with respect to delivering K-12 education. In fact, we suggest that the "leading edge" of K-12 education will be fashioned by educational entrepreneurs who can create and grow value in their organizations by covisionary "educational multisectorism" leveraging the comparative advantages of all three sectors. In other words, the most successful K-12 educational leaders will be "innovative, opportunity-oriented, resourceful, value-creating change agents" who pursue their social mission across sector lines. Both the problems and the opportunities associated with the current and future context of K-12 education call on the skill set of "educational leader as educational entrepreneur."

Examples of such cross-sector ventures already abound in K-12 education, even in the area of school operation. Regardless of the ultimate viability of such initiatives, schools districts have much to learn (and undoubtedly much of which to be skeptical) as they observe various entrepreneurial not-for-profit and for profit forays into all areas of their current responsibilities and functions. Many of these forays hopefully can serve as "laboratories" to model candidate best practices and innovative potential approaches with respect both to educational content and to educational delivery. As such, their results can provide invaluable guidance to inform and adjust both the division and the coordination of labor between the public school system and the not-for-profit and for profit private sectors so as to achieve the greatest overall benefits for K-12 learners. One can certainly debate whether such forays should or should not be happening (a different debate, as an earlier comment suggests, than the debate about "privatization.") However, such debate does little to advance the learning of our K-12 youth. In the spirit of finding opportunity in the disguise of problems, a more entrepreneurial question to ask is how organizations from the not-for-profit sector, from the for profit sector, and from the public sector can best pool their strengths through covisionary "multisectorism" to achieve simultaneously enhancements of performance outcomes and of social justice in the K-12 space.

References

Andrews, M., Duncombe, W., & Yinger, J. (2002). "Revisiting economies of size in American education: Are we any closer to a consensus?" *Economics of Education Review*, 21(3), 245-262

Beales, J.R. (1994). *Teachers, Inc.: A private-practice option for educators.* Los Angeles: Reason Foundation.

Beales, J.R., & O'Leary, J.O. (1993, November). *Making schools work: Contracting options for better management.* Los Angeles: Reason Foundation.

Dees, J.G., Emerson, J., & Economy, P. (2001). *Enterprising nonprofits: A toolkit for social entrepreneurs.*, New York: John Wiley & Sons, Inc.

Dees, J.G., Emerson, J., & Economy, P. (2002). *Strategic tools for social entrepreneurs.*, New York: John Wiley & Sons, Inc.

Dirkswager, E.J. (2002). (Ed.) *Teachers as Owners: A Key to Revitalizing Public Education.* Lanham, MD: Scarecrow Education Book.

Farrell, W.C., Johnson, J.H., Jones, C.K., & Sapp, M. (1994). "Will, privatizing schools really help inner-city students of color?" *Educational Leadership,* 52(1),72-75.

Education Week on the Web (the editors) (2002, May 9). E-defining education.

Heyne, P. (2000). *The economic way of thinking - ninth edition.* Upper Saddle River, NJ: Prentice Hall.

Hirsch, W.Z. (1991). *Privatizing government services: An economic analysis of contracting out by local governments.* Los Angeles: University of California, Institute of Industrial Relations.

Hula, R.C. (1990). Preface. In R.C. Hula (Ed.), *Market-based public policy (pp. xiii-xiv).* New York: St. Martins Press.

Hunter, R.C. (1995). "Private procurement in the public sector in education." *Education and Urban Review,* 27(2), 136-153.

Kourilsky, M. (1995). "Entrepreneurship education: Opportunity in search of curriculum." *Business Education Forum,* 50(10), 11-15.

Kourilsky, M. (1998). *Marketable Skills for an Entrepreneurial Economy.* White paper, prepared for America's Promise-Alliance for Youth

Kourilsky, M. (2001). *Basic Economics: A Common Sense Approach.* Dubuque, IA: Kendall/Hunt Publishing Co.

Kourilsky, M. & Dickneider, W. (1988). *Economics and Making Decisions.* St. Paul, MN: West Publishing Company, Inc.

Kourilsky, M. & Kourilsky, G. (1999). *Marketable Career Skills for Youth: Importance and Preparation.* Kansas City, MO: Ewing Marion Kauffman Foundation.

Kourilsky, M. & Walstad, W. (2000). *The E Generation: Prepared for the Entrepreneurial Economy?* Dubuque, IA: Kendall/Hunt Publishing Co.

Murphy, J., Gilmer, S.W., Weise, R., & Page, A. (1998). *Pathways to Privatization in Education.* Greenwich, CT: Ablex Publishing Corporation

Pinchot III, G. (1985). *Intrapreneuring.* New York: Harper and Row.

Taylor, M.A., Dees, J.G., & Emerson, J. (2002). "The question of scale: Finding an appropriate strategy for building on your success." In Dees, J.G., Emerson, J., & Economy, P. (Eds.) *Strategic tools for social entrepreneurs.*, New York: John Wiley & Sons, Inc.

Thomas, W.C. (1996, August 23). "County privatizes hiring of substitute teachers." *The Tennessean,* B1-2.

Tyack, D. (1974). *The one best system: A history of American urban education.* Cambridge, MA: Harvard University Press.

Wenger, D.A. (1994). "The idea of private practice." In D.A. Wenger (Ed.), *Enterprising educators as school partners: A manual for educator entrepreneurs and school officials.* Watertown, WI: American Association of Educators in Private Practice.

Yelich, C. (1994). "A private practice option for teachers? The time has come!" In D.A. Wenger (Ed.), *Enterprising educators as school partners: A manual for educator entrepreneurs and school officials.* Watertown, WI: American Association of Educators for Private Practice.

Library Recommendation Form

International Journal of Entrepreneurship Education (IJEE)

To the librarian:

I would like to recommend the IJEE to the library.

Name: ....

Title: ....

Department: ....

Tel: ....

Email: ....

Signature.. Date: .... / .... / ....

Volume 2: Academic Year 2003/2004

	USD	EURO	GBP
Institutional / Library Subscription	195.00	195.00	137.00

Prices include postage and packaging.

Please order from:
Orders Dept, Senate Hall Academic Publishing, PO Box 8261, Shankill, Co. Dublin, Ireland
Fax : North America 416-251-9845, Europe (Ireland) +353 1 282 3701
Email: orders@senatehall.com
For all enquiries call our UK office: +44 121 233 3837

Order online at http://www.senatehall.com

IJEE Volume 2: Order Form

Name: ....

Organization: ....

Address: ....

....

City: .... Zip/Postal Code: ....

Country: .... Tel: ....

Email: .... Fax: ....

Annual Subscription Rates: (please tick)

Institution/Library: USD 195.00 .... EUR 195.00 .... GBP137.00 ....

Personal: USD 110.00 .... EUR 110.00 .... GBP 75.00 ....

To order individual articles and copies of the IJEE see the Entrepreneurship pages of our website at http://www.senatehall.com/ijee.
Please enclose a cheque made payable to Senate Hall Ltd or include credit card details below:

Mastercard: .... Visa: ....

Number: ....

3 Digit Security Code: .... Expiry Date: .... /.............. /.................

Amount: ....

Signature: .... Date: .... /.............. /.................

Please fax or send your order to:

Journals Department   North America Fax: 416-251-9845
Senate Hall Academic Publishing   Europe Fax: (Ireland) +353 1 282 3701
PO Box 8261   For all enquiries:
Shankill, Co. Dublin   Tel: (UK) +44 121 233 3837
Ireland   Email: orders@senatehall.com

Order online at http://www.senatehall.com/ijee